Presented to:

From:

Date:

Best Inspirational Stories of the Year

HONOR HB BOOKS

Inspiration and Motivation for the Seasons of Life

An Imprint of Cook Communications Ministries • Colorado Springs, CO

Best Inspirational Stories of the Year
ISBN 1-56292-262-9

Copyright © 2004 by Bordon Books
6532 E. 71st St. Ste 105
Tulsa, OK 74122

Published by Honor Books,
An Imprint of Cook Communications Ministries
4050 Lee Vance View
Colorado Springs, CO 80918
www.cookministries.com

Developed by Bordon Books
Manuscript compiled by Shawna McMurry
Designed by Koechel Peterson & Associates

All possible efforts were made by Bordon Books to secure permission and ensure proper credit was given for every entry within this book.

Contents

Word from the Publisher

Dear Reader,

Best Inspirational Stories of the Year—this wonderful collection of stories has been a fun project for our team to conceptualize and work on. Our editorial research team spent many hours looking through books, newspapers, magazines, and Web sites for the best inspirational stories to share with you. These are the best inspirational stories that we have found this year. Our purpose: to bring inspiration, encouragement, hope, and motivation into your life. We could all use a little more of those things! Our plan is to introduce future volumes in the months and years to come.

If you come across any great stories that inspire you, we invite you to share them with us for possible use in future volumes of this series. You can send them to us at the address below, or e-mail them to us at bestinspiration@bordonbooks.com.

Best Inspirational Stories of the Year
c/o Bordon Books
6532 E. 71st Street, Suite 105
Tulsa, OK 74133

Don't forget to tell us where you found the story (please provide the name of the publication, page number, author, and title of the story), as this information is necessary in order to include it for consideration in future volumes. We hope that you enjoy all these stories, and that they inspire you to faith, hope, love, and all the good things God has in store for your life.

Sincerely,
The Publisher

Introduction

What makes a story inspirational? It is the effect it has on you, the reader. When you read an inspirational story you are motivated to change, to persevere, to dream new dreams, to move beyond what you know so you are able to accomplish the great things you now realize are possible. An inspirational story moves and exhilarates you, and the year's best inspirational stories will stir you more than any other stories you have read. We hope this collection of stories brings you all of those experiences and more with the turn of every page. So pick up this book and read stories that will capture your heart, lift your spirit, and enrich your life in ways you never dreamed were possible.

The true stories in *Best Inspirational Stories of the Year* all pack a powerful message and offer a spiritual pick-me-up. The world may be chaotic and discouraging, but these uplifting stories will restore your faith in people and in the divine Author of the most inspiring story ever written. Take a few minutes and brighten your day with the kinds of stories that will warm your heart, tickle your soul, and leave you feeling good.

The Woman Who Loved Children

BY MARTI ATTOUN

*I*RENA SENDLER KEEPS A PHOTO of "her Kansas girls" on the bedside table in her nursing-home room in Warsaw, Poland. She rests easier now that her story is in good hands.

And her story is an astounding one, as awe-inspiring as that of Oskar Schindler, whose courageous acts of Nazi resistance became a book and an Academy Award-winning film, Schindler's List, in 1993. But unlike Schindler, who received international acclaim, Irena Sendler's story was a footnote in history for nearly 60 years.

That all changed in September 1999, when three teenagers, half a world away at Uniontown High School in Uniontown, Kansas, were looking for a topic for a history contest. Elizabeth Cambers, Megan Stewart, and Sabrina Coons stumbled upon a mention of Sendler in a 1994 issue of a news magazine, in which she was listed among other non-Jews who risked their lives defying Hitler during World War II. As a Catholic social worker, the article said Sendler organized the rescue effort of 2,500 Jewish babies and children from the Nazi-controlled Warsaw Ghetto in 1942 and 1943.

"We thought it was a typo," recalls Cambers, now 18 and a freshman at College of the Ozarks in Point Lookout, Missouri. "We thought it was supposed to say she rescued 250 children, not 2,500."

Encouraged by their social studies teacher, Norman Conard, the girls selected Sendler as the subject of their National History Day project, a nationwide competition in which students research and present a historical topic in a medium of their choice before a panel of judges. Conard's students participate each year in the contest; he frequently challenges them to delve into subjects that teach the importance of tolerance and acceptance of diversity. Studying such events, he says, is crucial in a place like Uniontown, a 288-population rural community that has little diversity, and not a single Jewish resident.

Excited about what they had learned about Sendler so far, the girls kept digging. But information was scarce. An Internet search rendered one result: a reference to Sendler's courageous acts on the Web site of The Jewish Foundation of the Righteous in New York City. Although reams have been written about the Warsaw Ghetto over the last half-century, including Wladyslaw Szpilman's memoirs on which the Academy Award-winning film *The Pianist* was based, the girls could find only a couple of books on the topic in their local library. They promptly wrote the authors of these books for more information. One sent a thin pamphlet, which included a few more facts about Sendler—enough that the girls could write their entry in the contest, a 10-minute play they titled *Life in a Jar*.

"We sat down and brainstormed what could have happened using other history books that described the Holocaust and first-person survivor stories," say Stewart, now 18 and a freshman at Pittsburg State University in Pittsburg, Kansas. The high school of 122 students doesn't have a drama department, so Conard became the play's director and producer. Stewart laughs and says, "If this play had been about our acting ability, it wouldn't have gone anywhere. It's Irena's amazing story that people keep wanting to hear."

Life in a Jar opens in September 1939, when the Nazis invaded Poland. Sendler, now 93, was just 29 years old. She worked for Warsaw's social welfare department, which, in part, included operating canteens that provided meals and other services for orphans, the elderly, and the destitute. An only child, Sendler was influenced early by her father, Dr. Stanislaw Krzyzanowski, the only doctor in their town of Otwock (15 miles outside of Warsaw) who was willing to treat Jews during a 1917 typhus outbreak. Tragically, he, too, contracted typhus and died; Sendler was only seven at the time. But she never forgot her father's ultimate sacrifice. "I was taught that if a man is drowning, it is irrelevant what is religion or nationality," Sendler has said. "One must help him. It is a need of the heart." (Her words have been translated from Polish to English.)

Then in the fall of 1940, Sendler watched as the Nazis forced 350,000 Jews inside the Warsaw Ghetto, a 16-square-block area that was walled off and guarded. With each passing month of the war, the torment of the people locked inside intensified. They were dying of starvation and disease while unknowingly waiting for the Nazis to herd them into freight cars that would ultimately take them to their deaths in the gas chambers.

Sendler joined Zegota, the code name for the Council for Aid to Jews in Occupied Poland, an underground network founded in December 1942 by Adolf Berman, a psychologist and political leader, along with six other prominent scholars, religious leaders, and political activists. The precise number of Jews and non-Jews who worked with the secret organization is not known, but together they did whatever they could to help the Jews, such as forging thousands of birth certificates and other documents to give Jews safe Aryan identities, and raising money to funnel to Poles, who hid Jews in their homes.

Zegota asked Sendler to head up their operation to smuggle Jewish children out of the Warsaw Ghetto. But first she had to get inside. Because the Nazis were on guard against the spread of infections beyond the Ghetto, they allowed the Polish contagious disease department to deliver medicine to the Jews. A Zegota member working inside the disease department forged a permit for Sendler so she could work undercover as a nurse inside the Ghetto; her code name was Jolanta.

With the help of her ten "messenger friends," as Sendler called her colleagues, and dozens of volunteers, she organized the effort to sneak the children to orphanages, convents, and private homes in the Warsaw region. Children who were old enough to talk were taught to rattle off Christian prayers and mimic other religious behavior (such as how to make the sign of the cross) so they could live safely without arousing suspicion of their Jewish heritage.

Sendler and Zegota devised several methods and routes to smuggle children out of the Ghetto. Kids escaped on foot or in the arms of volunteers, through sewer pipes or basements with underground passageways. Many also escaped through the courthouse, which had entrances on both the Ghetto side and the Aryan side.

Other methods were more inventive. For instance, a trolley driver and Zegota member, when crossing from the Ghetto to the Aryan side, hid little ones in trunks, suitcases, or sacks under his backseat where the Nazi guards could not see. Another supporter, an ambulance driver, kept his dog beside him in the front seat and trained him to bark to camouflage any cries or noises from the babies hidden under stretchers in the back. Sendler also arranged for babies and children to be sedated and smuggled out with merchants in potato sacks under their loads of goods.

Sometimes, she even sneaked sedated children out in body bags, telling the guards that they were dead. The children were then taken to a safe place where they were met by more of Sendler's colleagues and escorted to orphanages, convents, or the adoptive homes Sendler had arranged for them.

Day after day, for about 16 months, Sendler persuaded parents and grandparents to hand over their babies and children, to give them a chance to live. The anguished good-byes are still vivid in her mind 60 years later, says Sendler, and pass before her eyes each night before she goes to sleep. "There were terrible scenes. One mother wanted a child to leave the Ghetto while the father did not. The grandma wanted; the husband did not. They asked, 'what was the guarantee?' What kind of guarantee could I give them?" She couldn't even guarantee that she could get past the guards.

Sadly, says Sendler, many parents could not be convinced to surrender their cherished children. As a result, they perished together, most at Treblinka death camp in northeast Poland. By the end of the war, fewer than 1 percent of the 350,000 Jews inside the Ghetto had survived.

Thanks to the efforts of Sendler and Zegota, an estimated 2,500 babies and children were saved. On slips of tissue paper, Sendler recorded the identities of every child she rescued. Whenever possible, she wrote down his Jewish name, his new Christian name, and new address. Most "foster families" were told that the children they were taking in were Jewish, but some were merely told they were war orphans without their religion being specified. The whole family would be killed by the Nazis if the children's true identities were exposed, so Zegota urged parents who knew the children were Jewish to lie and say they were orphans or relatives. (The children's expenses were paid by donations to Zegota.) Sendler buried the names in jars under an apple tree in a friend's garden in Warsaw (hence the play's name, *Life in a Jar*). After the war, Sendler hoped the children would be located and their true Jewish identities revealed to them.

On October 20, 1943, the Gestapo arrested Sendler—they had long suspected she was running a smuggling operation, and one Nazi had a file on her. One of her messengers was caught and tortured until she gave up Sendler's name and home address. The Gestapo interrogated Sendler, demanding information about the identities of the other rescuers and the children in hiding. But she refused to talk. "I was quiet as a mouse," Sendler has said, adding that she was beaten by the Gestapo until her legs and feet were broken. "I would have rather died than disclose anything about our operations." (Because Sendler received no medical attention, the beatings left her permanently disabled, and she has had trouble walking ever since.) She was then taken to Pawiak prison, where she was sentenced to be executed. "If I had died, the names in the jars would have been lost forever to the Jewish people," Sendler has said.

At the last minute, the woman who had rescued so many others was herself rescued. On the day she was to be executed, Zegota paid a hefty bribe (to this day, no one knows the dollar amount) to a guard who allowed Sendler to escape. The guard subsequently posted her name on public bulletin boards as one of the executed, essentially rendering her invisible to the Nazis. She then went into hiding in Poland, just like the children she saved.

When Poland was liberated a year and three months later in January 1945, Sendler returned to her friend's garden and dug up the jars. She turned over the list of names of the children she rescued to Zegota's Berman. Berman and other members of the group tried to locate many of the foster families after the war so they could finally reveal the true names and heritages to the children they took in. Because Berman died in the 1970s, the exact number of people who were informed is unknown. Sadly, most of the children had no parents or grandparents to be found; most had died at Treblinka. Conard and his students have a list of about 700 names of those rescued—given to them by Sendler, other child survivors, and that they found in a book written by Polish researcher and author Lucjan Dobroszycki. In the late 1940s, Dobroszychki took down the names from some copies of Sendler's original pieces of tissue paper. But those original pieces of paper—and the copies, which contain all 2,500 names—have never been found.

"Irena Sendler worked in a climate where murder was legal and rescue was a crime, where murder was rewarded and decency punished," exclaims Renata Skotnicka-Zajdman of Montreal, 76, who says that Sendler and Zegota saved her life. "Because of their goodness during a time of darkness, I live and have children and grandchildren."

After the war, Sendler would go on to marry Stefan Zgrzebski and have two children of her own, a son, Adam, who died in 1999, and a daughter, Janka, now 56. (Irena acquired the name Sendler when she married her first husband, whom she divorced before the war.) Sendler continued her career as a social worker in Warsaw, but she never talked openly about her rescue work. Poland was under a communist regime, and the postwar climate wasn't safe. For almost 60 years, her story was essentially lost to history.

Back in Kansas, the three teenagers were trying to locate their heroine, the inspiration for their play. They assumed that Sendler had died, since none of their research mentioned where she lived. So they asked The Jewish Foundation for the Righteous to help them locate her grave. To the girls' delight, the foundation informed them that Sendler was alive, but at 90 years old, in poor health. So in March 2000, six months after starting their project, the girls sent her a letter to the address that the foundation supplied. "We explained who we were, and what we were doing," says Coons, now 20 and a student at Kansas State University in Manhattan, Kansas. "We told her that we found her story amazing."

Sendler's response, handwritten in Polish, arrived three weeks later. The girls found a local college student to translate: "I am curious if you are an exception or if more young people in your country are interested in the Holocaust," Sendler wrote. "I think that your work is unique and worth disseminating. I am very eager to receive and read your play."

In a series of letters, Sendler answered the students' questions, and slowly the details of her remarkable story unfolded, and an international friendship was forged.

By this point, *Life in a Jar* had won first place at the state level of the National History Day project, and the story of its success was covered in local papers. Then, in April 2000, the students held a presentation at their school. They invited parents and other members of the community to watch the play and announced that they had actually found their Holocaust heroine. As the girls brushed away tears, so did many in the audience. "Everyone is touched by Sendler's story," says Stewart.

After the emotional performance at Uniontown High, the students were invited to perform *Life in a Jar* for church groups, nursing homes, and civic organizations in Uniontown and throughout southeast Kansas. Through their correspondence with Sendler, the teens learned that she lived quite meagerly. At each play, they set out a donation jar, symbolic of the buried jars of names, and asked for donations. Their first gift to Sendler was $3, which they told her to use for postage. "We found out later that she gave the $3 away to a children's home," says Coons. "That's just how she is."

Although they didn't win any awards when they traveled to Maryland in June 2000, to compete in the national contest, the girls' play was quickly gaining national attention. They were asked to perform for the staff at the Jewish Foundation for the Righteous, and requests came rolling in from around the country from other organizations that wanted to see *Life in a Jar*.

With Conard's guidance, the students revised the play, added more roles, and enlisted other students' help. In January 2001, the teens performed the revised *Life in a Jar* at a junior high school in Kansas City. One audience member, a local Jewish man, was so profoundly moved by Sendler's story that he raised money from other Kansas City Jews to send the girls to Poland to meet Sendler.

In May 2001, Cambers, Coons, and Stewart were on a plane to Warsaw. "We got there and saw all these television crews at the airport," says Coons. "We wondered who could be the celebrity on the airplane." (A friend of the project had tipped off a Warsaw newspaper about the students' arrival, and a two-page article heralded their visit.)

"It wasn't real until I actually met Irena," says Stewart. "We all ran up and hugged her. She wanted to just hold our hands and hear about our lives." They kept a translator busy with questions back and forth about their families and schoolwork.

One by one, the girls held Sendler's hand and cried. Cambers told her, "I love you. You are my hero. You are my inspiration."

Sendler, a 4-foot-11-inch woman who now uses a wheelchair, deflected their praise. "A hero is someone doing extraordinary things," she told them. "What I did was not extraordinary. It was a normal thing to do."

To the girls, she paid compliments. "You don't sow seeds of food, but seeds of good. Try to make the circle of good that surrounds you grow bigger and bigger."

Sendler's friends took the girls to visit the places they had brought to life in their play: a concentration camp, the secret meeting room for Zegota, the apple tree where the names were buried. Sendler also introduced the girls to one of the babies that she saved: Elzbieta Ficowska, 60, of Warsaw. Ficowska was rescued at 5 months old by Sendler, who hid her in a toolbox, which was carried past the guards by a carpenter and Zegota supporter. Ficowska was adopted by a Polish woman. At 17, she learned that she was Jewish and that a friend of her adoptive mother's, Irena Sendler, had saved her life. Her biological parents had tucked a silver spoon in the toolbox with her first name and birth date; they both were killed by the Nazis.

Today, love and gratitude have come full circle, as Ficowska cares for Sendler in the Warsaw nursing home. She and the Kansas teens have become close friends and work together on spreading Sendler's story.

Before leaving Poland, the students gave Sendler a giant heart-shaped card the students in Uniontown had made for her. And fittingly, Sendler gave each of the girls a heart-shaped pendant, which they wear today as a reminder of how one person can make a profound change in the world.

Indeed, these three teens have. Thanks to the international

attention the girls have brought to her story, Sendler has received numerous awards for her courageous work. After learning she was to be given a $10,000 humanitarian award from the American Center of Polish Culture in Washington, D.C., she wrote to her girls: "My emotion is being shadowed by the fact that no one from the circle of my faithful co-workers, who constantly risked their lives, could live long enough to enjoy all the honors that now are falling upon me . . . I can't find the words in order to thank you, my dear girls. Please be aware that all the honors that now I am receiving from many parts are only due to your merit. Before the day you have written the play, *Life in a Jar*, which you are presenting constantly, nobody in my own country and in the whole world cared about my person and my work during the war . . . I hold you close to my heart. Irena-Jolanta loves you very much."

Four years later, the project continues. The three original girls, now all in college, have entrusted a new crop of students with Sendler's story. Today, 17 students are involved in the project as cast members and researchers. The Sendler archives at the Uniontown High School include some 3,000 pages of research notes, about 75 letters and e-mails from Sendler (several Polish friends of Sendler's receive e-mail from the students on Sendler's behalf and ferry them to her so she can answer within a day or two), and hundreds of other e-mails from fellow teachers, audience members who were moved by the play, and even those who believe they could be one of Sendler's children. Conard spends two hours each day answering these letters. Students set up a Web site, www.irenasendler.org, with information about their upcoming performances, details of Sendler's life, and photographs of her and Uniontown students. The site gets about 1,000 visitors each month.

Keeping the Sendler story alive is no longer just a three-person project; it's a community effort. Uniontown declared November 7, 2001, Irena Sendler Day. Parents have sewn costumes for the play and driven students thousands of miles to more than 100 perform-ances in eight states. Enough donations have been collected since the beginning of *Life in a Jar* to cover many of Sendler's expenses in her Warsaw nursing home.

In one letter, Sendler thanked the students for their ongoing efforts. "You have done big work for all the world, your homeland, Poland, and for me. I warmly believe that you will always go the same way, to stop wars and evil at last. And goodness will win." [1]

Bethany Hamilton Emerges from Tragedy with a Message of Hope

THE BRIGHT HAWAIIAN SUN glistened on the water, warming Bethany's back as she paddled her surfboard out to catch a gentle morning wave. The exhilarating feeling of the ocean's pulse was nothing new to this thirteen-year-old champion surfer or to her companions—best friend Alana Blanchard, Alana's father, and brother. Bethany was surfing with them on the morning of October 31, 2003—a day that would change Bethany Hamilton's life forever.

Lurking in the water below Bethany was a fourteen-foot tiger shark. In a sudden attack, it emerged from the water and bit off her left arm just four inches below her shoulder.

Alana's father, Holt Blanchard, described the next moment to a CBN reporter: "All of a sudden Bethany goes, 'I got attacked by a shark!' And she wasn't panicking or anything, so I almost thought she was kidding. She was paddling toward me. I was probably 20 feet away. And then I saw a bunch of blood in the water."

While Holt tied a surfboard leash around the remaining part of Bethany's arm to slow the bleeding and helped her paddle back to shore, Bethany prayed. "I might not be here if I hadn't asked for

God's help," Bethany told a local reporter. "I look at everything that's happened as part of God's plan for my life."

After two surgeries, the resilient teen was on her way to recovery and adjusting to life with only one arm. Hospital officials said that as soon as Bethany was able to walk, she visited other patients to offer them hope and support.

While many would see the loss of an arm as a crushing blow to an up-and-coming surfer, ranked number eight in the world and planning on a professional surfing career, Bethany sees things differently. "I kind of realize that it's given me an opportunity to, like, witness for Him, and more people will want to talk to me since I'm that girl that got attacked by a shark. So they'll want to hear what I say. And that's pretty good."

Even before the accident, Bethany had made it a priority to glorify God through her surfing, writing scriptures on her board before competitions, such as "I can do all things through Christ who strengthens me." The youth leader at her church, Sarah Hill, describes Bethany as a sensitive girl who "didn't like people being picked on." Hill said of Bethany, "If there's any kids being left out, she would take care of that kid, stand up for that kid. If it was a new girl, she'd go and be with her. She didn't need to be in a clique. Wherever she was, was cool."

After visiting with Bethany since the attack, her pastor, Kahu Stephen Thompson, commented, "I think she's always had a heart for God. I have the feeling that the experience she's gone through has brought this out even more. She had that faith and that hope all along, but it seems to have increased."

While Bethany continues to use the events of October 31, 2003, as a platform for sharing the faith and hope she finds in God, she has far from given up on her dream of becoming a professional surfer. In less than a month after the attack, she was surfing again, and three months later she was competing.

In an interview with CBN, Bethany boldly stated, "I can say one thing. [God] definitely got me through this. And I have a special verse—the first verse a friend of mine gave [to me] when I was in the hospital: 'For I know the thoughts that I think toward you, says the Lord. Thoughts of peace and not of evil, to give you hope—a future and a hope'" (Jeremiah 29:11).

Bethany holds firmly to her faith as she presses toward a goal much higher than the hovering waves she attempts to conquer. One of her friends said, "I think Bethany's faith is simple. She's not preaching, you know, this huge gospel. She's just preaching this faith that she has in God; that He's her strength, and that everything that's happened is part of His plan."

That simple faith is reaching thousands around the world. Her support Web site gets hundreds of hits each day from loving supporters offering messages of encouragement and wishes for Bethany's success as a surfer. But perhaps best of all are the countless messages from people telling Bethany how her testimony has changed their lives. This thirteen-year-old is certainly making her mark as a powerful force; not only on the water, but also in the lives of everyone she touches. [2]

Don't Let Me Die!

BY CARLY BOOHM AS TOLD TO GAIL WOOD

I GOT UP EARLIER than usual that chilly Saturday
morning in April. I had a fun weekend ahead, and I didn't want to
miss any of it. My youth leader and several friends from my youth
group were heading to the Wenatchee River to take part in a relay
race. I wasn't going to be in the race—I'd never even been in a
canoe before—but I did get to be involved as a volunteer. My job
was to take the canoes and paddles from point to point along the
river in the car.

"Now remember, you're to stay out of the river," my mom
reminded me for about the hundredth time as I left that morning.

"Don't worry, Mom," I said, driving off to meet my friends in the
church parking lot.

Off we went, singing songs and talking as we headed toward
eastern Washington. Before long, we started talking about the next
day's Ridge to River Relay, an annual competition in the
Wenatchee Valley. The race starts with skiers zipping down from
the top of Mission Ridge and ends with people paddling down the
Wenatchee River.

Finally, we arrived at the river, and someone suggested we go canoeing. My friends weren't experienced white-water canoeists, but I knew they had some canoeing experience. Besides, we'd only be floating for about two miles. So I called my mom and asked for permission. I told her we were going to put the canoes into the water right in front of a park. Reluctantly, she said OK.

My mom later told me that when I had described the water, she had figured it was a gentle, flat, lake-like area of the river. Actually, the rushing water was higher than usual because of heavy rains and melting snow from the surrounding mountains.

Carefully, I stepped into the aluminum canoe along with Ruben and Marya—two of my best friends. Excited, we pushed off from shore and began what was supposed to be a short—and safe—trip.

We didn't go very far before the canoe overturned, dumping us into the freezing waters. The swift current quickly pulled us down-river. We swam to a little sandy island and Ruben pushed the canoe to shore.

I was starting to realize that this ride would be far more difficult than I'd imagined. "I don't want to get back into that canoe," I protested, shivering. I was scared. But we still needed to get back to the other side of the river, where we'd started. And since we'd never be able to swim across the swift waters, the canoe was our only choice.

"Come on, Carly," Ruben insisted.

Reluctantly, I climbed back in. As we approached a bridge, we suddenly turned sideways. Ruben shouted to Marya to paddle harder, but we were sucked toward a pillar of the bridge. We hit it hard and the canoe capsized, throwing Ruben and Marya into the river. They were swept downriver and were able to struggle to shore.

But I got stuck under the overturned canoe. The force of the water had wrapped it around the pillar like tinfoil. I was pinned about three feet underwater. I couldn't break free or raise my head above the water. My lungs ached for air.

I was trapped.

As soon as they made it to safety, Ruben and Marya began screaming for help.

My body was pinned under the canoe, but I managed to lift my hand in a plea for help. Shocked bystanders on the bridge could barely see it above the rushing waters. Someone called 911.

It was 2:50 in the afternoon. A frantic race to save my life began.

Meanwhile, Everett Gahringer, a volunteer for the sheriff's department, was running his boat upriver. He saw people on the bridge frantically pointing at me and the submerged canoe. Someone in his boat reached out to me, but we couldn't touch.

I was drowning.

"Please, God, save me," I prayed. "Don't let me die."

Mr. Gahringer wrapped a rope around the canoe I was still trapped under and tugged, hoping to jar me free. But it was useless.

Another sheriff's boat arrived—one with a much more powerful motor. But the river was still too powerful. Mr. Gahringer went to shore, thinking it was over.

It was now 3:15, and I had been underwater for 25 minutes.

Everyone thought it was too late to save me. But one medic on shore had been praying that they could free me. That medic, Shawn Ballard, knew the icy waters would slow my body functions. That would extend my chances of surviving. He knew I might be able to go a little longer without air.

"Let's try again," Mr. Ballard yelled through cupped hands.

Then a fire truck with a winch and cable rolled onto the bridge. Volunteers wrapped the cable around the canoe. Slowly, the canoe rose, and my body was freed. My body was quickly swept downriver. Mr. Gahringer revved his motor and raced down to pull me in.

It had been 45 minutes since our canoe flipped and trapped me underwater. I still wasn't breathing, and my heart had stopped.

Inside the ambulance, Mr. Ballard used shock pads to restart my heart. Several times. It started. Stopped. Started. Stopped. "God, please save this girl," he prayed.

My body temperature was 72 degrees when I arrived at the hospital.

My parents drove four hours to the hospital, praying the whole way. When they walked into the intensive care room, I was still unconscious. The doctors told my parents I probably wouldn't live through the night. If I did, I'd be little more than a vegetable.

Four days later, I slowly raised my arm and waved to my mom, who was sitting by my hospital bed. Mom cried. It was a miracle. I was alive.

Whenever people hear my story, they talk about what a miracle it is that I'm alive. The governor of Washington named me the "Miracle of the Season." Larry King interviewed me on his television program, and my story has been on *Dateline NBC*, *The Today Show* and the *It's a Miracle* program.

And it's true: The fact that I am alive is a miracle.

But my recovery wasn't over. It's been a long journey. I was in the hospital for two-and-a-half months after the accident. I've had to learn almost everything again—how to speak, how to walk, how to read. After I left the hospital, I had to go to physical, occupational and speech therapy regularly.

My short-term memory has suffered as a result of the accident, but I returned to school that fall for my senior year. I was able to graduate as salutatorian of my high school class, though, and that was a real victory for me. I attended a community college for a while, and recently transferred to a four-year school. My memory is improving, and I'm studying to become a doctor, which is what I wanted to be even before the accident.

I've always shared my faith in Jesus and invited people to come to church with me, and I've had a lot more opportunities to talk to others about Him since the accident. My dad says God spared my life so I can tell others about His love. So I try to do that whenever I can.

Sometimes when somebody becomes a Christian, people say they got "saved." I like to think God has saved me not just once, but twice. [3]

It Isn't Whether You Win or Lose...

BY IRA BERKOW

O N A RECENT SATURDAY morning, on the home football field of the Somers Middle School, here in this quiet town about an hour's drive north of New York City, the coach of the Somers team of primarily seventh graders called a play to begin the second quarter. He had alerted the opponents, John Jay Middle School, as well.

It was hardly something that Vince Lombardi or Bill Parcells might do. But when Bud Von Heyn, the Somers coach, met before the game with Jeff Tepper, the John Jay coach, to go over the ground rules, Von Heyn said: "I need a favor from you." Tepper listened, and agreed.

"O.K., guys, line up," Von Heyn told his young players, in their red jerseys and white pants and silver helmets, on the sideline. "We're going to run the E. J. Shuffle."

Then Von Heyn shouted across the field to the John Jay coach. "Here we go, Jeff."

And Tepper, who had explained the plan to his team before the game on Oct. 18, passed the word to his team.

The play, which would start on the John Jay 35-yard line, was going to be run for E. J. (Eugene Joseph) Greczylo, a 15-year-old eighth grader who had come into the game for the first time—it would be the only time—and was instructed where to position himself in the backfield.

"Remember," Von Heyn told E. J., "follow the fullback. He'll do your blocking."

And so on this lovely fall day, with the flush of brightly colored trees as background, and a modest, but enthusiastic, crowd of parents and friends looking on in the bleachers, the ball was snapped to the quarterback, who then handed it off to E. J. E. J., the husky lad with the gentle face and an intense but slightly wobbly running style, tucked the ball beside his belly, made his way toward the sideline, and then turned upfield toward the goal line.

"Go, E. J., go!" came shouts from the Somers side of the field— and the players who stood along the John Jay bench.

E. J.'s blocking teammates barely touched their opponents, but the opposing players, giving chase, seemed to fall or trip or lunge and, with arms outstretched as though they were about to embrace a long-lost friend, repeatedly missed the ball carrier by wide margins.

"The John Jay kids were really into it, maybe even overacting a little," Von Heyn said with a smile. "And when I talked to Jeff after the game, he told me that, yes, he thought his players should get Academy Awards."

Behind all this was the effort to make one kid feel good, to make him feel a part of things. And that kid was E. J. Greczylo, who has Down syndrome, but who had desperately wanted to be on the football team, who had not played in the team's first game the week before and was disappointed.

"When he told me he wanted to play football," said Katie

Greczylo, E. J.'s mother, "I thought it wasn't a good idea." Her other child, her son, 12-year-old Alex, was in the kitchen at that moment, and her husband, George, was at work. "Alex said to me: 'Mom, you're always telling us to follow our dreams. Well, football is E. J.'s passion—this is his dream.'"

"But Alex," I said, "What if someone hurts him?"

She said Alex responded: "E. J.'s a big boy. He could hurt someone, too. I know. I'm his little brother."

Katy Faivre, who teaches the eight children—five of whom have Down syndrome—in a class for disadvantaged seventh and eighth graders at Somers, and who has been E. J.'s teacher since the second grade, said: "In this school, we try to treat the disadvantaged kids as though they are like everyone else. For the most part, they do what the others in the general education do. E. J.'s been in two school plays, he's in the marching band—plays the bass drum. The kid thinks he's a kid."

She added: "As long as you explain to the other kids that the disadvantaged students have certain disabilities, they listen. We make it comfortable for them to ask about it, and the stigma disappears."

In the school corridors, other students hail E. J. as they do any of their other classmates. "Hey, E. J." "What's up, E. J.?" And in his somewhat muffled articulation, E. J., with short blond hair and his book bag strapped on his back, responds in kind, as he heads for football practice.

Down syndrome, a genetic condition that affects an estimated one in 1,000 births in the United States, includes varying degrees of mental retardation.

"The way we feel about E. J.," said Matt Corning, a teammate, "is that he's one of us, part of the team. It feels no different than anyone else. And the E. J. Shuffle? We practice it. So everyone is cool with it."

Von Heyn said: "What amazed me is that when we do something like the Shuffle for E. J., you don't hear the normal grumbling from the other players that you might expect. It's like they look forward to it."

The collaboration that allowed E. J. to score a touchdown was not unique. An article in *Sports Illustrated* a year ago depicted a similar effort in Ohio involving a handicapped member of the high school football team. That youngster was 17 at the time, two years older than E. J.

Katy Greczylo said that when E. J. was born: "We never could have dreamed that all this would happen for him.

"He's exceeded all our expectations, with the help of this incredible school, and the Special Olympics, which also gave him confidence in the sports he participated in. And this football thing—when you think of all the troubles with sports and football that you read about like the hazing, the overemphasis, this brings you back to what it ought to be about. And the kids that were involved, they'll never forget this. It changes all our lives."

And when E. J. crossed the goal line, he was greeted with congratulatory slaps on the helmet and endearing bumps and high-fives from his teammates. The John Jay players, Von Heyn recalled, some still on the ground from their futile tackles, observed all this with broad smiles.

"My kids are still talking about it," Tepper said. "On the bus back after the game, they were asking me, 'What's Down syndrome?' It was a great learning experience."

The touchdown didn't count, though E. J. wasn't aware of that, and John Jay won, 16-12.

"But E. J. was so pumped with the touchdown," his mother

recalled. "And he tried to find me in the bleachers: 'Mom, Mom!' And he put his thumbs up. It blew me away. He looked like just a regular, typical kid out there. And when he came home, he said: 'Dad, I made a touchdown! I made a touchdown!'"

And what did her husband say?

"You mean," she said, "after he wiped away the tears?" [4]

Prayer Convoy on Interstate 70

BY RON LANTZ

RAFFIC ON I-70 wasn't too bad. I should have been enjoying myself that day last October, sitting up in the cab of my 18-wheeler, cruising through the Pennsylvania hills.

Thirty-six years as a trucker, and I still got a kick out of my rig. Bass Transportation bought this 600-horsepower tractor in 2000. I was the only one who drove it, and although I'd logged almost 400,000 miles, the cab was still so clean you could eat off the floor. If traffic held steady, I would make my usual run right on schedule, hauling a tanker of building compound from Ohio to Delaware, then deadheading back to my home in Ludlow, Kentucky.

But I didn't make the run on time that day, for the same reason I wasn't enjoying the trip. The Beltway sniper. The words hammered in my head. Eight dead and two wounded already and it didn't look like there'd be an end to it. At any truck stop in the D.C. area, all we talked about was the white van the police were looking for. Schools were closed, people too scared to leave their homes. It weighed on me that this guy was out there getting ready to kill again. I knew what it was like to lose someone you love. Five years earlier my wife, Ruth, and I had lost our only son, Ron, to multiple sclerosis.

It was a pretty October day just like this one when he died. I knew when I got to the nursing home that something was up because there was a lot of hollering down the hall. "What's going on?" I asked.

"It's your son, Mr. Lantz," a nurse said. I hurried to Ron's room. There was our boy sitting on the edge of his bed, hands raised over his head, praising the Lord. For more than a year, he hadn't been able to sit up on his own.

"I'm leaving here," Ron said. "Someone's coming through that door tonight to take me home." Then he looked at me real hard. "Dad, I don't want to be up in heaven waiting for you and you don't make it."

It wasn't the first time he'd brought up the subject. Ron was a real committed Christian. My parents raised me in the faith, but somehow I'd drifted away. "I want you to go over to my church right now," Ron went on. "Find my pastor and give your life to the Lord."

Well, that's exactly what I did. Afterward I went back to the nursing home and told Ron. I'm glad I had the chance, because Somebody did come for my boy that night to take him home.

My life turned around. I got active in church. I headed the men's fellowship, led retreats, and was on the Sunday school board. I'd never start a run without kneeling by my bed at the rear of the cab and asking God to watch over Ruth.

After the sniper shot his first victims, I'd been praying about that too—that someone would stop this killing spree. It had gone on for 12 days already. Around 7:00 P.M., when I was about an hour and a half out of Wilmington, Delaware, the usual report came on the radio. Nothing new on the sniper. All they knew was that a white van might be involved.

I got to thinking about what I'd learned at church, how a bunch of people praying together can be more powerful than a person praying alone. *What if I can get on my CB, see if a few drivers want to pull off the road with me and pray about this?*

I pressed the button on my microphone and said that if anyone wanted to pray about the sniper, he could meet me in half an hour at the eastbound 66-mile-marker rest area. A trucker answered right away. Then another and another. They'd be there. I hadn't gone five miles before a line of trucks formed, some coming up from behind, others up ahead slowing down to join us. The line stretched for miles.

It was getting dark when we pulled into the rest area. There must have been 50 rigs there. We all got out of our cabs and stood in a circle, holding hands, 60 or 70 of us, including some wives and children.

"Let's pray," I said. "Anyone who feels like it can start." Well, the first one to speak up was a kid maybe 10 years old, standing just to my left. The boy bowed his head: "Our Father, who art in heaven. . . ."

We went around the circle, some folks using their own words, others using phrases from the Lord's Prayer. It seemed to me there was a special meaning where it says ". . . deliver us from evil. . . ."

The last person finished. We had prayed for 59 minutes. All those truckers adding an hour to their busy schedules!

Ten days later, October 23, I was making my Ohio to Delaware run again. There had been another killing and the sniper was no nearer to being caught.

Right from the start, there was something different about my trip. In the first place, it was a Wednesday. I normally made my runs Tuesdays and Thursdays. But there was a delay at the loading dock so I told my pastor I'd have to miss our Wednesday night prayer meeting. "We'll be praying for you," he said.

The second thing that happened: I was stopped by the cops. Once was rare for me. This trip I was pulled over three times. Not for very long, they were just checking papers, but it made me late getting into Wilmington.

The next strange thing: Instead of catching a few hours of sleep, I headed back west as soon as my cargo was off-loaded around 11:00 P.M. That wasn't like me at all. I knew too many sad stories when a driver didn't get enough sleep. It was like I had an appointment, like I couldn't sleep even if I tried.

At midnight the Truckin' Bozo show came on the air, a music and call-in program a lot of truckers listen to. There was news in the sniper case. There were two snipers, not one, and police now believed the guys were driving a blue 1990 Chevrolet Caprice with New Jersey plates, license number NDA-21Z. Not the white van we had all been looking for.

I wrote down the tag number. Just before 1:00 A.M., I reached the rest stop at the 39-mile marker near Myersville, Maryland, only a few miles from where so many of us had made a circle and prayed. Westbound on I-70, this was the only rest area between Baltimore and Breezewood with a men's room. I wasn't going to pass that by.

And here was the last weird thing about that trip. The truck aisles were full. I'd never seen so many rigs at that stop, drivers asleep. Only thing I could do was swing around to the car section. I wouldn't be long. Climbing down from my cab, I noticed a car in the No Parking zone. The light over the men's room door was shining right on it.

A blue Chevrolet Caprice.

There must be hundreds of blue Caprices out there. I looked closer: two men, one slumped over the wheel, asleep. Beyond the men's room was a row of bushes. I crept behind them and squinted to make out the license number. Jersey plates. N . . . DA2 . . . 1 . . . Z.

Quiet as I could, I climbed back in my rig. Better not use the CB in case those guys have one. I punched 911 on my cell phone. "I'm at the Myersville rest stop. There's a blue Chevrolet Caprice here, Jersey license NDA-21Z."

The operator asked me to hold. In a minute she came back with instructions. Wait there. Don't let them see you. Block the exit with your truck if you can.

If an 18-wheeler can tiptoe, that's what mine did. I blocked as much of the exit ramp as I could, but there was still room for a car to get by. Five minutes passed. Only one other driver was ready to roll. Soon as I told him what was happening, he pulled his rig alongside mine, sealing off the exit. I sat in my cab, looking out the side mirrors at that blue Caprice, expecting a shootout, thinking I ought to be scared and wondering why I wasn't.

Five more minutes passed. I was afraid another truck or a car would drive up and honk for us to move it, waking the suspects, but no one stirred. The cops slid up so quiet I didn't know they were there until suddenly it was like the Fourth of July with flash-grenades lighting up the night to stun the two men.

FBI agents, state troopers, officers from the sheriff's department swarmed the rest stop. Searchlights. Breaking glass. Shouts. The thump of helicopters, SWAT teams in night-vision goggles, running low, crouching, guns drawn.

Next thing I knew the two men were being led away. The police took down names at the rest area. It was two and a half hours before we were free to go. Since I'd been blocking the exit, I was the first one out.

Five miles down the road I started shaking so bad I could hardly hold the wheel. Then I got to thinking about all the unusual things that had to happen for me to be at that place at that time, and about my friends at church praying for me that same evening. And I couldn't help thinking about my son, Ron, who'd led me to that church.

I looked in my rearview mirror at the lines of trucks behind me and remembered leading another line of semis 10 days earlier. I remembered the circle of truckers and their families, holding hands, voices joined together to pray, ". . . deliver us from evil."[5]

The Silver Saint

BY GRACE FOX

HELENA PETERS, 77, of Campbell River, British Columbia, packs her suitcases for her seventh missionary journey to Kenya in seven years, eager to visit the ministry to African street children that she founded. Each trip lasts three to six months. She smiles at raised eyebrows and well-meaning comments such as, "Is this a good idea at your age?"

"God can use anybody who's available to Him," Helena says. "He equips the obedient to do His will. I'm living proof."

The gray-haired grandmother of nine travels alone. "Alone with God," she stresses.

"I'm not afraid to go. I've only had a few scary moments, like when someone flashed a switchblade in my face, and when I was robbed, and when rebel forces burned my house. But God is faithful! I've never lost a suitcase. I've not been sick more than a day or two in the last seven years." She breaks into a familiar melody: "My God and I walk through the fields together, we walk and talk as good friends should and do . . ."

Indeed, God has walked with Peters, overcoming a myriad of obstacles throughout her life to bring her to this point. Peters

recalls growing fearful of the dark when her family escaped Soviet
Russian persecution in 1929, fleeing in terror night after night.
After emigrating to Canada, she lived in poverty as the "dirty thir-
ties" waged war against her father's farm. A poor diet left her with
rickets, making walking difficult. Allergies plagued her. Poor eyesight meant wearing thick glasses.

"I thought I was so ugly I felt sorry for anyone who looked at
me," says Peters. "I refused to look in a mirror when I combed my
hair because I didn't want to see myself. I didn't think I had anything to offer anyone."

Beneath the battered self-worth, however, lay a heart longing to
serve God in Africa. As a young Bible school graduate, Peters
spoke with a missions representative about the possibility of serving overseas. He asked about her health. When she explained her
limitations, he said, "Don't bother applying." A year later, she
approached a representative from a different mission board. Again
she heard, "Don't bother applying."

Despite Peters' disappointment, her passion grew for Africa. For
nearly 50 years she financially supported missionaries. She prayed
faithfully for the Africans, especially the continent's children.

During that time, Peters focused on raising her three children
and maintaining a difficult 39-year marriage. Her husband suffered
with schizophrenia. After his death in 1995, she prayed, "Lord,
what do You want to do with the rest of my life?"

The answer came: Declare the Gospel to others. Within three
months she'd sold her mobile home, a 26' RV, and her car. She was
free to go.

When Peters touched African soil several months later, she was
healthier than she'd ever been, accepted by the second mission
board that had refused her. "I've never told them that they rejected

me 50 years earlier," says Peters. "At 20 they turned me down. At 70 they accepted me!" Peters shakes her head, laughing at the irony.

Peters was used to working with the poor, having volunteered in Mexico, Nicaragua, and Hawaii years earlier. But nothing had prepared her for the desperate scenes she faced in Nairobi.

"One day I walked past a steaming garbage heap. I turned my head away from the stench," she says. "Suddenly I noticed movement and realized there were children searching for food. I saw a little girl, maybe four or five years old, sitting in the middle of the trash heap, eating a rotten orange."

Peters and several colleagues sprang into action at the sight of a boy sprawled on the road waiting to be run over. "He was addicted to glue, tired of scrounging for food, tired of living," she says. "We pulled him off the road just in time." Peters says she knew their actions saved the boy's life that day, but unless they did something else, he would repeat his suicide attempt.

Within two days they had established a feeding program at a nearby church that agreed to let them use the premises. Local vendors donated cooking utensils and rice. Peters paid for vegetables. At first, 26 street kids came. The numbers soon swelled to 80. Most were between the ages of 8 years and 20 years. Peters seized the opportunity to provide more than physical nourishment.

"We invited the kids to come early in the mornings," she says. "We sang songs and had Bible lessons. One of our helpers taught them to play baseball. That proved interesting—they weren't used to playing on teams or with rules so fights broke out quickly!"

Peters also recognized the need for basic health-care instruction. When the kids requested pancakes for lunch, she agreed on one condition. "I'll cook pancakes on Saturday," she said, "but before you eat, you have to be clean." When Saturday arrived, the children were given soap and provided with a place to wash.

Eventually she and Kenyan pastor Simon Mondo founded "Overcomers Caring Ministries," an independent ministry for street children. Many of the young people were orphans; some were runaways. "One of the problems we see results from Kenyan men having more than one wife," explains Peters.

"A man stays with the wife he likes the most. When she has too many children, he abandons her for another wife. She's left with all these children and no way to support them. The woman often turns to prostitution to earn money. Often the older kids are kicked out and told to bring food. Many times they simply leave home."

Ten-year-old Mina was a runaway. Living in the slums for seven years, he was addicted to glue and destined for early death. One day he responded to the Gospel presented by Pastor Simon who led a weekly outreach team to central Nairobi's dangerous streets. He returned to live in a room Peters had rented for street children.

"He changed drastically," says Peters. "A year later, two women from his hometown showed up at one of our church programs. When Mina walked in, one of the women recognized him—she was his aunt!"

The women carried the good news of Mina's well-being to other family members. His mother came to see for herself, and she, too, received Christ as her Saviour. Mina returned to his hometown as an evangelist.

Realizing the benefit of getting kids off the streets, "Overcomers Caring Ministries" is building an orphanage to provide permanent housing for up to a dozen children at a time. Property was donated. The foundation has been laid and walls will soon be erected. Peters is trusting God to provide funds for a clean water supply. A medical doctor has volunteered free services, and certain medications are dispensed at no cost.

Peters' passion for sharing about the Gospel is expressed in countless ways. For instance, expenses such as building supplies, book shipments, salaries for seven full-time staff, and the street children's food are paid largely from her seniors' pension. She writes and self-publishes poetry to help cover costs.

Each time she visits Nairobi, she presents the Good News through song and puppet presentations in public schools. "The first time I visited one particular school, I spoke to more than 700 students at once," she says. "Now the student population is more than 1,000. Last year the principal invited me to speak to that group twice. When I said I wanted to come back every week, the principal gave me my own classroom! There's more religious freedom there than in North America."

Peters openly presents the Gospel several times a day. "I always take peppermint candies along to pop in my mouth when my voice starts to give out," she says, chuckling.

Concerned that new believers grow in their faith, she wrote 21 discipleship lessons, taught by Pastor Simon. She established a reference library for pastors in Kenya, and a well-stocked library in Zaire with hundreds of donated books.

Her zeal continues back in Canada. Every Friday her modest mobile home becomes a refuge for a half dozen women struggling with issues such as rape or eating disorders. Peters treats them to steaming homemade blackberry tea and teaches them truths from God's Word. She writes songs about God's love and, strumming on her omnichord, teaches them the lyrics. "It really helps them know they have a God who loves them unconditionally," she observes.

"I'm never out of work," she says with a laugh. "I'm busier now than I ever was.

"I love seeing changed lives," says Peters. "I love seeing the glow of the Lord in people who had given up on life. You know, I was just a poor farm girl with many health problems, but that didn't matter to God. He uses and equips anyone who's willing to be used."[6]

The Best Inspirational Quotes

A marriage may be made in heaven, but the maintenance must be done on earth.

—ANONYMOUS

It is better to be silent and be considered a fool than to speak and remove all doubt.

—ABRAHAM LINCOLN

The greatest act of faith is when man decides he is not God.

—OLIVER WENDELL HOLMES

Swallowing angry words before you say them is better than having to eat them afterwards.

—ANONYMOUS

Happiness is a perfume you cannot pour on others without getting a few drops on yourself.

—RALPH WALDO EMERSON

A skeptic is a person who, when he sees the handwriting on the wall, claims it is a forgery.

—MORRIS BENDER

For peace of mind, resign as general manager of the universe.

—LARRY EISENBERG

The Circuit Rider

BY GRACE FOX

*L*IKE THE CIRCUIT RIDERS of bygone days, Robert E. Harris, 79, of Asheville, North Carolina, reaches people with the Gospel message wherever he rides his horse. For example, take Friday night at the speedway. Moments before the races begin, the loudspeaker crackles to life with lyrics of "The Circuit Riding Preacher," to the familiar tune of "The Battle Hymn of the Republic." A surprised hush replaces the sounds of manmade horsepower and cheering spectators, as eyes focus on a horse and rider sauntering before the stands.

Looking as if plucked from the frontier landscape, Harris, perhaps North America's last practicing circuit riding preacher, approaches wearing a black frock coat, a 10-gallon hat, string tie, and cowboy boots. Harris' presence commands respect. Thousands sit quietly, listening to the Good News presented through his simple invocation and dedication prayer.

Harris' forerunners a couple of centuries earlier took God's Word on horseback to the taverns, chapels, gambling halls, and log cabins of the early American frontier, preaching salvation by grace through faith in Christ alone to settlers of the young nation's dense backwoods and stark prairies. Wherever people gathered, the preachers preached.

Tonight Harris, who has never married, speaks at a racetrack. Tomorrow it might be at the local flea market, a county fair, a seniors' home, or a low-cost housing project.

Sunday mornings find him preaching three services at a nondenominational drive-in church held in a shopping mall parking lot. Venues vary in keeping with his predecessors' mission to preach the Gospel where it is not often heard. Whatever the arena, the message remains the same: God loves you and has a plan for your life.

Harris has recorded memoirs about his career, which began in 1940. He writes his purpose: "My circuit rider ministry is intended as a follow-up to what my brethren in the past have done. I serve the same Master as they [did].

"Conditions are different from frontier days but the gnawing emptiness of men's souls seems only to have intensified rather than eased by improved physical surroundings. Therefore, I have dedicated myself to Christ to ride a circuit of preaching places so that mankind and God may be reconciled. . . . My motto is 'Reaching the masses with the message of the Master.'"

Harris responded personally to the Gospel message as a 15-year-old. His faith grew as he read a New Testament, sitting beside a country road while grazing his cow in the pasture nearby.

"I decided to do whatever the Bible said to do and leave off whatever it said to leave off," says Harris. "The first thing I knew, I was giving up things I'd gotten accustomed to, and I was taking up things I'd never dreamed about taking up. One of them was going to the local jail because Scripture said, 'When I was in jail you visited me.' I felt a lot of fear and timidity and hoped I wouldn't have to go more than once.

"The sergeant on duty asked who I had come to visit. I told him I didn't know anybody; he could give me whoever he had. As well as a teenage boy could do, I gave my witness to the inmate, then walked away thinking, *Thank the Lord I won't have to do that again.* That was 60 years ago; I'm still doing jail visitation."

Harris preached his first sermon at age 17. Sitting in the yard of a tiny shack beside a railroad track, eight people sang and listened to him teach from Scripture. Of the eight, four placed their faith in Jesus Christ. Before long Harris was leading prayer meetings, preaching in open-air services held in people's yards, and conducting tent meetings.

In 1949, a radio minister asked Harris to take over his program. Harris agreed. By 1956, besides continuing in radio, he began broadcasting a Sunday afternoon television program called, "The Story of Jesus." At one point, Harris developed a horseback-riding circuit preacher theme for his radio program. The introduction featured supporting music and sound effects to imitate a horse's clomping hoofs, followed by a brief devotional. Twenty-six stations aired the program for several years before Harris began rethinking the potential of using the theme for evangelism.

In 1979 Harris bought the appropriate attire, printed brochures offering his services, borrowed a horse, and launched the outreach. The biggest obstacle he faced was overcoming the fear of what others might think of him.

"Pride gets in the way," he says. "Imagine going out in a 10-gallon hat, a long-tailed coat, and cowboy boots. People look at you like you're from Mars! Some people make fun and joke. After you've endured that and proved yourself, they begin to respect you and think there's something to it."

Eventually Harris purchased a quarter horse named Two-Eyed Redeemer. When that horse died nine years later, he purchased two Tennessee Walkers—Sunduster and Sundance.

Wherever Harris appears by invitation—state fairs, museums, horse shows, amusement parks, college campuses—he and his horse attract attention. Children especially love to pet the animal. "He gets the hide rubbed right off his nose!" says Harris with a chuckle.

Like his forerunners, Harris carries Gospel literature in his saddlebags—3,000 brochures, to be exact. He gives the printed material to all who will receive it. His message is down-to-earth. After briefly describing the historical circuit riding preachers, each brochure tells the story of Tsali, a Cherokee brave who gave his life for the sake of his tribe in 1838. It explains that a greater sacrifice was made on behalf of all mankind through the death and resurrection of Jesus Christ.

The pamphlet's five-point message is plain for the reader: God has not forgotten you, He knows how you feel, He knows where you are on the road of life, He knows what you've done, and He loves you anyway. It ends with the question, "What are you going to do about it?" and a prayer of salvation. Harris has distributed as many as 50,000 pamphlets per year at rest areas along North Carolina's interstates, giving away as many as 2,000 in two hours. Sometimes up to 15 people at once surround him, asking for literature. Although he's no longer allowed to bring his horse with him to the rest areas, his unique attire attracts the attention of weary travelers who stop to stretch their legs.

"People from around the world come through here," he says. "One day within two hours I spoke with folks from Hong Kong, Pakistan, and New Zealand. I'll probably never be a foreign missionary, but if I stay here long enough, the world will come to me."

Harris' evangelistic approach has created opportunities to speak with people of varied backgrounds—a European ambassador, a serial killer, the president of a national tire company, motorcycle gang members, national politicians.

Harris faces mixed receptions, just as his frontier predecessors did. Although he hasn't been run out of town by disgruntled saloon keepers upset that the preacher's message has disrupted their livelihood, he has faced hecklers jeering, "Ride 'em cowboy!" when his horse refused to cooperate. He has been teased for his ministerial clothing. He's been criticized for his five- to seven-minute presentation at the races. But although some responses are negative, Harris says they are far outnumbered by the positive.

Harris admits sometimes wondering if his efforts are accomplishing anything worthwhile. "When those thoughts come, I'm reminded that God's Word will not return void but will accomplish what He desires (Isa. 55:11). That helps keep me going," says Harris.

Occasionally he receives encouraging feedback. He recalls one day, when a traveler approached him at a restaurant and asked, "Are you the Circuit Rider?"

Harris answered, "Yes, sir."

The man said, "While I was listening to a Christian radio program not too long ago, a man from San Diego was being interviewed. In the course of the interview, he said he was converted after reading a brochure given to him by a circuit riding preacher in western North Carolina."

Harris received a visitor on his 79th birthday. During their conversation, the man told him that he had placed his faith in Christ during one of the open-air meetings Harris had held 60 years earlier.

"How many lives have changed as a direct result of my witness is unknown to me," Harris writes in his memoirs. "God keeps the records. My intention is to be a channel of Christ's love to others. My own life is blessed and my horizons continually lifted for I see no limits to what God can do through anyone yielded to Him. It can truly be said that the Circuit Rider ministry takes God to men by witnessing and brings men to God by winning them."

The frontier days are gone. The venues have changed. But Robert E. Harris continues to fulfill the original mission as he carries the unchanging message to the masses.

The times may change, as may the appearance and communication methods of people who live to present the Gospel to others. But the message itself remains the same: God loves us, forgives sin, and gives a meaningful life to those who submit to Him.[7]

Signs of Love

BY CAROLYN CAMPBELL

THE TWO GIRLS with the brown pageboys both love to draw. Sitting in her feeding chair at home in Salt Lake City, 3-year-old Lucy Coleman, who suffers from cerebral palsy, bangs on the tray to get her sister Leah's attention. Leah, 6, who is deaf, asks in sign language, "What color do you want?" "Purple," Lucy signs back. When Leah replaces the colored pencil in her sister's hand with the dark purple one, Lucy, gracious as always, signs, "Thanks."

"They're just typical sisters," says their mother, Rachel Coleman, 28. But the fact that the girls can "converse" is nothing less than a miracle—of her own making. She had taught American Sign Language first to Leah and then Lucy, hoping that Lucy's mind, if not her body, was intact. Coleman's instincts were right: She discovered her disabled daughters not only could communicate with each other, but the world, and that sign language could benefit healthy children as well. "It's the most incredible thing watching the girls," she says. "There's a feeling in your heart that's indescribable."

Back in early 1998, when Leah was 13 months old, Coleman, a stay-at-home mom and a musician, singer and songwriter, and her husband, Aaron, 31, who was at college studying to be a city parks supervisor, were concerned that their baby had yet to utter a sound. Their doctor told them not to worry unless Leah didn't speak by 15 months. But the next week, when Coleman's mother asked her to call repeatedly to Leah while staying out of sight, the child never responded. "My heart sank," says Coleman. "I realized she'd never heard a story I read or a song I sang."

Diagnosed with a profound hearing impairment, Leah began wearing hearing aids, but still couldn't hear well enough to communicate solely through speech. Coleman gathered stacks of books and videos on sign language, taught herself the rudiments in four weeks, and began teaching Leah the words a toddler would normally be learning. (Deaf infants typically start sign language between 10 months to 12 months.)

Leah was a quick study: Within a month, she had mastered 70 signs. "She could sign 'airplane' when other kids her age would just point at one," recalls Coleman. "Instead of just whining when she was hungry, she could tell me she wanted milk or crackers." Coleman says that mothers of perfectly healthy infants who observed her and Leah "stopped me everywhere—the post office, the grocery store, the bank"—saying they, too, wanted to sign with their babies.

"One day we were waiting at the pharmacy when a row of five kids were staring at us," Coleman recalls. "Leah signed, 'Why are people always staring at me?' I said it was because she could do something they couldn't." Coleman began teaching American Sign Language at her church and at local preschools, but the demand became greater than she could handle. That's when Coleman began making her own video to teach parents and children, hearing or deaf, how to sign.

In the meantime, Coleman's sister Emilie, 32, whose son Alex was born the week that Leah was diagnosed, had immediately begun teaching him sign language so he could communicate with his cousin. "One day, when he was 9 months, Alex was crying and tugging on Emilie's shirt because he wanted to nurse," recalls Coleman. "Suddenly, he stopped, looked up at her, and signed 'milk.'" It was then that both mothers realized that babies, whose fine motor skills develop sooner than the complex muscle coordination required for speech, can sign before they can talk.

In October 1999, Coleman became pregnant, and an ultrasound at 18 weeks revealed the baby had spina bifida, a cleft in the spine that causes paralysis below the affected vertebra. Coleman decided to undergo intrauterine surgery to try to repair the damage. She raised $15,000 with the help of neighbors, friends and family, and had the one-hour procedure when she was five months pregnant. When Lucy was born in May 2000, the couple was overjoyed to find she could move her legs, feet and toes. "The doctors told us to take her home and treat her like a normal child, because that's what she was," says Coleman.

But by 9 months, Lucy was unable to urinate and was losing control of her body. "She held her fists tight and had her head thrown back, but other than that she was like a rag doll," says Coleman. "Her legs were floppy and couldn't bear her own weight." The diagnosis was devastating: cerebral palsy. Lucy couldn't crawl or speak, and showed no emotion; a year later, doctors concluded she was also mentally retarded.

True to character, her mother was undeterred: "Though she was locked in her body," she says, "I knew Lucy was in there." In March 2002, Coleman, who had not touched her guitar since learning Leah was deaf, wrote a song, "Show Me a Sign," that was a prayer for her baby. The creative vision helped her to complete the sign-language video she had envisioned that would be more engaging that the ones she had learned from. Coleman wrote more songs and a script with Emilie's help, and asked a former colleague with a production company to shoot the 30-minute film, *Signing Time*, which starred Leah, Alex and herself, and came out in April 2002.

A month later, Coleman was playing the video at home when she heard a small voice say, "Wa-wa." She bent over Lucy's crib and watched in wonder as Lucy signed, "water." Coleman soon discovered Lucy could sign all 18 words in the video, which meant both her disabled children would be able to talk to each other. "It was one of those 'Aha!' moments," she recalls. "I thought, *This is going to work. We can cross this bridge.*"

Today, Lucy knows her ABCs and colors and can sign hundreds of words; she loves to chatter all day long with Leah and her parents. Coleman had already made two more videos, and sells some 2,500 of them a month through her own Web site, www.signing-time.com, and Amazon.com. Her husband has become a stay-at-home dad, enabling her to promote her videos at parent organizations, trade shows and conventions for the deaf. "One mom told me her daughter, who can hear perfectly, goes to sleep holding the video," Coleman says.

She and her daughters reap the blessings every day. "Which shape do you want me to draw—circle, square, star or heart?" Leah signs to Lucy. "I want a star," Lucy signs back. And Leah draws it for her.[8]

Learning to Walk with Faith

BY GINNIE GRAHAM

$\mathcal{A}$T THE STRINGFELLOW HOUSE, Faith walks. In fact, Faith—the dog—walks and runs just about everywhere, despite being born with only two working legs. She walks upright, like a human being.

Faith is not just a name for this 7-month-old mixed breed. "We had faith she would walk again," said 14-year-old Laura Stringfellow. "We had faith in her. And that's her name."

The Stringfellow family in Oklahoma City believed a disabled puppy should have a chance at a normal life. They worked in shifts nursing the puppy through her early weeks. They put her on a skateboard to show her how movement feels. They watched her learn to roll from side to side at 5 weeks old to running full sprints now at 7 months.

"I knew she would be special," said mother Jude Stringfellow. "Maybe people will say, 'Hey, I don't have to have a perfect dog, but I can get one that is happy.' And Faith is certainly happy."

The family adopted Faith when the original owners were going to put her to sleep. The owners feared the congenital disability would leave her immobile.

"No dog deserves to die," said 17-year-old Reuben Stringfellow. "She was a very normal little puppy; a real strong and normal puppy with two legs. She was a cripple as a puppy, but I wanted to hold it, pet it, feed it and take care of it."

Faith can maintain perfect balance and sits on her haunches. She has a smaller, useless front limb that has atrophied, and is scheduled to be amputated next week.

"I thought she would crawl the rest of her life," said Reuben Stringfellow. "I'm real proud of her."

Slightly taller than 3 feet, Faith can be an imposing creature to fellow pets. Cats scurry under furniture when the Godzilla-like chow and Labrador mix darts up to play. "The pets treat her like any other animal, but the cats are scared of her," said Laura Stringfellow.

Faith has a loving fascination with fire stations and firefighters, often sprinting at the site of either.

For fun, Faith takes walks with her family, tussles with the other family pets, chases the cats and plays tug-of-war with a sock.

A corgi helped goad her into walking by yapping at her from across a room and at times nipping her heels.

She joins a family filled with two other dogs, three cats, a couple of hamsters and a snake or two.

"She's a rough-and-tumble type of dog," said Jude Stringfellow. "We call her Tyrannosaurus rex because she'll stand up to get the height advantage and bite on their necks or dive to bite their heels. I think our corgi regrets showing her how to herd and nip."

On a recent trip near a pond, Faith experienced her first swimming lesson when she jumped in the water. "She was in over her head and looked like a mermaid," said Jude Stringfellow. "We pulled her out like a marlin; she dried off and jumped right back in." Faith repeatedly jumped into the water, trying desperately but unsuccessfully to swim.

"There was this moment after the fourth or fifth time we pulled her out, when she went too far. She gave us a sad look and realized she couldn't do it."

But there's not much else Faith can't do.

She likes moving pillows to the couch before pouncing on it and loves attention, often whining until someone pets her. Faith is housebroken, and stands by the door with a whimper when she needs to be let outside. She uses the bathroom standing up, and rests on her legs to eat.

"She plays hard and she sleeps hard," said Jude Stingfellow. "And she's a spoiled dog. We call her the diva because sometimes she won't perform when we want her to."

Faith's story has circled the globe through stories in Canadian, Swedish, Mexican, French and Dutch tabloid newspapers. A story appeared recently in the National Enquirer and the British Broadcasting Corp.

The family would like Faith to be trained to help disabled people, but they will not give her away. "We'd like for her to be an inspiration," said Jude Stingfellow. "I've prayed and told the Lord I want Faith to work for Him."[9]

An After-Christmas Gift

BY LEE KNAPP

ONE OPPORTUNITY I did not want to miss at Christmas was to serve dinner at a homeless shelter downtown. After being relegated to the church's substitute list in September, I jumped at the chance when a friend called to say she'd need me one Wednesday in mid-December. Besides wanting to get better acquainted with members of a new church we'd been attending, I had been longing for a more tangible experience of faith to round out my spiritual resumé. For too long my faith had been living in my head, with no other work to do but memorize facts about God and figure out my personal life.

Indeed, my head had become a lively Parisian salon to which a variety of voices paid regular visits. Jesus had come in recently, commanding me, "Feed my sheep," while an aging Miss America reminded me to "help people," if only to impress the judges. More often, especially since the month when I'd passed my 45th birthday, the conversation was dominated by the topic of death—specifically, mine.

After miscues in both December and January, waiting in vain for fellow church members to join me at two homeless shelters with the same name, I was more determined than ever to do my selfless good works, even if for selfish reasons. Those mishaps, which had seemed like a supernatural test, turned out to be a kind of scavenger hunt for an after-Christmas gift God had hidden for me.

On a freezing night in February, I finally found myself at Freedom House, standing behind a long table, serving up cornbread. As more than 100 people came in from the 20-degree weather, they walked along with their trays and thanked us often. One man was handsome, except for a few missing teeth, and could have been a basketball star or banker in another time. Then came a huge man with beautifully chiseled facial features, wearing not only a knit hat but also a bulky scarf knotted on the front of his forehead, making him look like a swami or one of the three wise men. Another short, timid man with thin strands of hair plastered over his scalp in a severe left-to-right orientation shuffled by, muttering the whole time he was there, "I should be in the hospital. They wouldn't let me stay."

I was feeling a certain lightness of heart. In fact, I hadn't thought about death the whole evening. Then a tall man with a voice like a sports broadcaster came up to the serving table, directly in front of me. *Would he want something? Should I think of something spiritual to say?* Instead, he asked, "Hey, are you all Christians?" Like a modern Elijah, in his wonderfully clear voice, he began his story.

"I want to tell y'all what happened to me. It was September 10, 1999. I was in North Carolina lying on my bed. I know I did not fall asleep. This was not a dream. An angel came to me to show me heaven. Man, you guys, it was real. I'm telling you, it was real. There was a river, a huge river, flowing right through the middle of where I was walking, and it flowed into a fountain but never flowed out. There were lots of buildings, real architecture that was mostly white and beautiful, huge, man. You know how Jesus says 'In my Father's house there are many mansions'? Well, it's true. There are houses in heaven. And the angel was showing me around. I recognized her because it was the same one—like she was my guardian angel—who came to me 15 years ago when I tried to commit suicide. Both times I told her I wanted to stay there, but she said it was not my time. I'm telling you, guys, it was real. I didn't want to come back here, but it wasn't my time. And there were people there, not really flesh and bones, but there were men and women and children. They were kind of clear, but everyone was like a bronze color, kind of see-through bronze or something. You could definitely recognize people."

His voice began to crescendo, slightly preacher-like. His tone was prophetic. "Heaven is real, man. I'm telling you. So you gotta' keep on doin' what you're doin'. It's all worth it. Keep on doin' what you're doin'."

You could have driven a truck through my slacked jaw. The picture he painted of heaven was so vivid and somehow strangely resonant, and his enthusiasm was infectious. Call me naive or soft-headed, but I didn't want to relegate this man's vision to the effects of a substance or mental illness, even if that were the case. I didn't care. I chose to suspend my rationality and enter into the imaginative promise and hopefulness of what he shared. After all, the birth of Jesus sounds a little crazy, too.

The man next to me spoke first. "Have you written this down for your family?" Our prophet looked blankly at him, but with a twinge of interest while buttoning his old Navy pea coat.

I broke in and said to him, "You know, I really needed to hear you tell me this tonight. I've been worried too much about dying. Thank you. It really helped me." He looked at me and again said,

"Just keep doin' good. Keep doing what you're doin'." Again, my church friend said to him, "You really need to write your vision down."

Then it hit me. I am a writer—sometimes. I looked up at him and asked, "What's your name?"

"Derek," he answered, by now prepared to go out into the weather, his backpack in place and holding a piece of cardboard.

"Thanks, Derek, for telling me this. I'm pretty sure I was supposed to meet you tonight. I'll write it down for you."

Those of us from church swept up, got our coats, and headed downstairs to the back parking lot. I was still a little stunned and wasn't able to tell my friend Connie what had happened yet. We crept up the alley in my minivan, and ended up right next to the sidewalk in front of the shelter. Among many of the others we'd just served, there stood Derek, right next to us at the passenger window, holding a cardboard sign.

For some inexplicable reason, I very consciously and quickly looked away from him, focusing instead on the approaching traffic to my left. I just felt so useless all of a sudden—and ashamed of my self-importance and tightly wound brain. But maybe that was a good starting-over point, a way for faith and hope to come back to life. I also may have avoided any eye contact because the scary truth about our common humanity—especially on a 12-degree F. night—hit me hard as I saw him there. That may help, too, to nudge my earlier misdirected intentions about good works into a more true line, and action. "Just keep doin' what you're doin'."

Once I pulled out into traffic, I did catch a glimpse of the sign he held: HOMELESS, PLEASE HELP.

I keep thinking about Derek's vision, letting my imagination take me there to see those buildings we're promised, trying to distinguish the faces in bronze that I may know, to hear the flow of the river. God knew I needed Derek's vision. I'm glad for whatever selfish reason or Spirit-led impulse that prompted me last Christmas season, so I could be in the right Freedom House at the right time minding the cornbread to hear about it.[10]

Charity's Children

BY ELIZABETH GEHRMAN

*I*T'S 2:00 P.M. ON A FRIDAY, and the graduate students shuffling into room 238 at the John F. Kennedy School of Government building at Harvard University have a lot on their minds. They face a final exam in one of their toughest subjects: macroeconomics. One of the students, an attractive 29-year-old with the unlikely name Charity Bell, has something extra to worry about: picking up an infant. "I know it's today," she says. "And all morning I kept thinking, *Please, God, not before 2:00 P.M.*"

Mercifully, it's 5:30 before she gets the call from Boston Medical Center to pick up Brian,* her newest baby. In what has become a familiar routine, she makes her way to the newborn nursery, breaking into a huge smile as a nurse hands her the tiny baby, wrapped in a hospital blanket. A foster parent, Charity is on perpetual standby, taking in abandoned or abused infants and toddlers and caring for them until a parent can claim them or until the Department of Social Services (DSS) finds permanent placement with relatives or adoptive parents. Brian is her 38th charge in four years.

"Hello, stinky," Charity coos as she cradles the six-day-old baby.

---

* *Children's names have been changed to protect privacy.*

"How are you, sweetheart? Are you going to come home with me? Yes, you are! Oh, you're just a little sweetie boy, aren't you?" She sits in the ward's rocking chair, cuddling Brian, as the nurses fill her in on his condition.

There is a lot to take in. Brian was born premature and addicted to cocaine. His mother, a homeless drug addict, left the hospital as soon as she was medically cleared. She has several other children, all in adoptive homes. The hospital staff and DSS personnel reached out to the mother but concluded that she would not be able to provide a safe environment for her baby. Brian's father is unknown, and no family members stepped forward, leaving the newborn a ward of the state of Massachusetts.

Brian is irritable, as are many babies addicted to cocaine, with the typical withdrawal symptoms of muscle tension and shakiness. His eyes roll upward severely, his arms flail, and he's probably in some pain as well. Some babies born addicted to drugs suffer developmental delays—how well they catch up depends on the quality and stability of the care they receive in the first few years.

Charity holds Brian very close, rocking him gently and murmuring to him in her soothing alto. After a little while, she dresses the newborn in a blue onesie from Baby Gap with a matching striped knit cap, and the two of them leave the hospital.

"He was so thrilled to be held and cuddled," Charity says later. "As soon as I picked him up, I could just feel him relax and settle down." He settles down so well, in fact, that Charity feels comfortable keeping her dinner date that evening, meeting with eight friends at a restaurant in Harvard Square, in Cambridge. "I always try to go back to my normal life," she explains. "If I were to stop everything every time I got a baby, I'd be doomed."

Throughout the evening, Brian sleeps in the arms of Charity's dinner mates, waking occasionally for a bottle-feeding before drifting off again. Charity's friends fuss over him whenever he wakes, but for the most part, their conversation revolves around school and professors, boyfriends, and plans for the weekend.

Amazingly, Charity also works part-time, baby-sitting for others and doing bookkeeping and odd jobs—all while attending one of the nation's most demanding graduate schools full-time, maintaining an active social life, and becoming a new mom over and over and over again. One day she wants to have her own children— "bunches and bunches of them." Right now, she doesn't even have a steady boyfriend. But her days are filled with babies, and very particular ones at that. Charity specializes in HIV-positive and drug-addicted newborns, who, in addition to the usual discomforts of being thrust into a bright, loud, and unfamiliar world, are often sick. She lives on caffeine. But despite the challenges—and despite knowing that she must give up the babies within a few weeks or months—she is smitten by every single one she takes in.

"All of a sudden you feel this thud in your heart," she says. "When you first meet them, you're like, OK, it's a baby. Kinda funny-looking. And then you wake up in the middle of the night to feed them. They cry, you pick them up, you lock eyes with them, and you fall in love. It's incredible."

Charity's babies go everywhere with her. The dark-haired young woman with an ever-changing child is a familiar sight at the Kennedy School. When she has an exam or a quick errand to run, she rarely lacks for willing baby-sitters. It's a school dedicated to public service, so naturally everyone is supportive of Charity. "But even in the group of do-gooders at the Kennedy School, Charity stands out," says Joseph McCarthy, the school's senior associate dean. "She's kind of a Mother Teresa figure with a sense of humor."

"It's difficult for people to comprehend how hard it is to do what Charity does," says her friend and fellow student Amy Lovell Kelly, whose mother took care of a foster child when Amy was growing up. "I always feel that the kids who get Charity as a foster mom are lucky. They're suffering, and she changes them completely in a relatively short period of time. And she makes it look easy."

Which is particularly remarkable because so much of Charity Bell's own life has been anything but easy.

It's a toss-up which was less likely for Charity: becoming a Harvard student or a foster mom. "I am definitely not supposed to be at Harvard," she says flatly. Charity and her younger sister, Faith, grew up poor in Ledyard, Connecticut, a small military town. They never knew their father; their mother was, as Charity puts it, "a wonderful woman who tried real hard but had severe alcohol abuse" problems. When she could, Charity's mom worked odd jobs; but, for the most part, the family lived on public assistance and town food pantries.

Charity's high school chorus director, Jamie Spillane, remembers her well. "She was in a tough situation and trying to deal with what was going on with her mother," he says. "She broke down a lot in school. The girls' home life was just completely and thoroughly unstable, and Charity came to school because school was stable. It was something she could grasp on to." Still, he says, even then he knew "she was a special kid. She saw all the things that can be bad if you let them, and she just made a pact with herself that she was going to be different."

Faith Bell attended school more sporadically. She found her passion in horses, and today, newly married, lives on a farm in rural North Carolina, where she handles contracting for tobacco farmers and goes horseback riding whenever she can. "There's something in both of us that is very strong, and I'm not sure what it is," says Faith. "Our mom was able to make us realize we could stand on our own two feet. There are a lot of things we did without, but we didn't take it as a defeat. We didn't sit back and say, 'I wish I had this, I wish I had that.' We both wanted to accomplish something."

Charity knows it's easy to draw comparisons between her life and those of the babies she mothers. But there's an important difference, she insists: "My sister and I were deprived of real things, but we were never deprived of love. My mother loved us, worshiped my sister and me, which is what made us. You can do a lot with love."

Thanks to her magnificent singing voice and the encouragement of Jamie Spillane and his wife, Linda, Charity became the first person in her extended family to go to college, attending the New England Conservatory of Music on a scholarship. But during her training as an opera singer, she realized that "I wasn't going to be able to spend my life just concentrating on me. I know it sounds cheesy, but I owed too much to Jamie and Linda and to the other people who had made sure my life was going to be OK." She wanted to give something back, and toward the end of her college years began volunteering with various organizations.

Just after Charity graduated from the New England Conservatory of Music, her mother died of an asthma attack after years of battling alcoholism and heart disease. She was 44. "Something in me clicked that you don't live forever," says Charity. Volunteer work seemed to be what mattered most, and the Peace Corps an obvious next step.

After spending 20 months in Guinea, West Africa, working on HIV-AIDS education and infant malnutrition, Charity returned to New England, her zeal for helping others stronger than ever.

She found her niche on the pediatric floor at the Tufts-New England Medical Center, in Boston, volunteering to cuddle babies, spend time with kids with cancer, whatever was needed. That's where she met Lucy, a "lonely, lonely two-year-old who clung to me for four nights in a row." Charity was shocked to learn that Lucy was a foster child stuck at the hospital because there were not enough homes to go around.

It was then that she decided to become a foster parent—even though the state's ten-week-long training course and background check prevented her from taking Lucy home. By the time Charity was ready, Lucy had been placed elsewhere.

Her first real charge, Isaiah, arrived a short time later, one day old and weighing just over four pounds. He was also addicted. That first night, Isaiah became ill and wound up in the neonatal ICU. Charity stayed at the hospital with him for three days and nights, sleeping in a folding chair beside his bassinet. "The doctors said, 'You're just the foster mom—go home. We'll call you when he's better.' But I could not imagine leaving this little person by himself in the hospital." Once Isaiah was released, Charity kept him for three months, taking him with her to work and going on with her regular life, just as she does today.

When she gets her master's degree in public administration from Harvard this month, Charity would like to start a nonprofit organization to recruit and support foster parents. She's already picked out a name—Foster the Future—and, with her usual efficiency, has created a Web site that will be up and running by late spring, Fosterthefuture.org. "I know that every baby I take care of has the potential to be amazing," she says, her voice thick with emotion. "It's important to make sure that they have love and affection and care."

With Isaiah, her first baby, Charity experienced the pain that comes with that love and care. "When he first left," she says, "I was devastated. I was the first person he smiled at. I picked him up when he was crying. I took him to the doctor. I was his mom!" Even after all this time—and despite knowing it's the best thing—Charity never takes it in stride when she must part with an infant. "But a caseworker told me that it's in the first three months of a baby's life that he learns what love is," she says, "and that's what has gotten me through the last 37 kids. If I can teach them a little bit about love, they'll recognize it when somebody gives it to them."

Little Brian seems to recognize it already. Six weeks after she first cradled him in the hospital, Charity sits in the cafeteria at the Kennedy School, chatting with friends and looking after the baby in her quiet way, feeding him while her own lunch grows cold. She smiles when a French exchange student stops by to shower him with kisses. Brian shows none of the drug-withdrawal symptoms he had in the first week, but at nine pounds, he is still a bit small for the fleece snowsuit she bought him. (The $14 a day she is paid by the Department of Social Services barely keeps the babies in diapers, so Charity uses her own money for each baby's wardrobe.) To her satisfaction, the baby boy's cheeks have grown chubby and his chin has doubled since she brought him home.

"Oooooh . . . so fat!" she says, holding Brian up and snuggling nose to nose. "That's what always make him laugh." For Brian's part, he holds tight to Charity's finger and sucks on her neck, nuzzling into her sweater and fastening his gaze on the person he truly adores, the one who has taught him everything he knows about love. [11]

The Best Inspirational Quotes

If you want to be a leader with a large following, just
obey the speed limit on a winding, two-lane road.
—CHARLES FARR

An atheist is a man
who has no invisible means of support.
—JOHN BUCHAN, LORD TWEEDSMUIR

Devoting a little of yourself to everything means
committing a great deal of yourself to nothing.
—MICHAEL LeBOEUF

One reason the dog has so many friends: he wags his
tail instead of his tongue.
—ANONYMOUS

The next time you feel like complaining, remember
that your garbage disposal probably eats better than
30 percent of the people in this world.
—ROBERT ORBEN

To know the will of God is the greatest knowledge, to
find the will of God is the greatest discovery, and to
do the will of God is the greatest achievement.
—ARNOLD H. GLASOW

That Boy Was Me

BY RAY GIUNTA

COUNSELING PEOPLE IN CRISIS has been my life since I finished Bible college in 1987. I was there after the 1989 Loma Prieta earthquake in the San Francisco Bay area. I've helped students who have survived school shootings. I was on the scene at Oklahoma City in 1995. But nothing could have prepared me for what I'd find in New York City in the wake of the terrorist attack on the World Trade Center. Shaken by the specter of death and destruction on an unimaginable scale, I had to wonder if one man could really make a difference in the face of so much suffering. Could any of us?

I was up early on the West Coast that day, on my way to a 6:00 A.M. meeting in Sacramento, when I heard something on the car radio about a plane hitting the World Trade Center. It took a morning of rumors, sound bites and television images to clarify what was actually happening on the East Coast. We feared the worst as rush hour came to a head at 9:00 A.M. California time— some of the hijacked planes were still unaccounted for. But the targets that day turned out to be confined to the East Coast. Physical targets, that is. Every American had been hit emotionally.

I wanted to get to New York immediately. But I'd trained myself to wait for an invitation from some group. Disaster sites are always chaotic, and help—even professional help—has to be organized if it is to be effective. I also believe that God directs me through these invitations to the places where I can do the most good.

I packed my bags so I'd be ready. "Meeting in the kitchen," I called to my family. My wife, daughters and son crowded around the table. "I might have to go away again for a while, but I don't want you to be scared." I looked at Katie, my younger daughter, sitting across from me, and leaned in toward her. "Remember, what can you count on?"

"That you'll be back as soon as your job's done," she said with confidence.

"That's right. I'll be back soon."

I always made a point of saying that. A seven-year-old should know for sure she can count on her parents. That was not the case in the house where I was born in Trenton, New Jersey, in 1960. My truck driver father drank up his pay instead of feeding and clothing his wife and nine children. My mother had problems of her own. Dad eventually went to prison for failing to support us. By that time, we were living hand-to-mouth on welfare. One day Mom just walked out the door, supposedly to get a loaf of bread.

Hours passed. No bread. No Mom.

My oldest sister, who was 10, took charge. She tucked me, the baby, into an open bureau drawer, and fed us whatever food she could scrounge up. When the cupboards were completely bare— one week after our mother disappeared—my sister went out and knocked on a neighbor's door to ask for help.

We stopped being a family that day. My brothers and sisters were sent to foster homes. I was hospitalized, near death from malnutrition and infection. Dad died a few years later of cirrhosis of the liver. We never knew what happened to Mom. I was adopted by the Giuntas, the only family I knew until I was 27.

That was when my wife got pregnant the first time. Her doctor encouraged us to find out everything we could about my family medical history. At the time, I was a criminal investigator for the state of California. I could have laid my hands on the information a hundred different ways. But I'd had my reservations about learning the truth. "It's for our child," my wife encouraged me.

A 1960 Trenton, New Jersey, phone book showed three listings for Lanigan, the name of my birth parents. One of them was my uncle. One call led to another, and on Easter Sunday 1986, the nine of us were reunited. The older siblings talked about the fear, the heartbreak, and the confusion of being abandoned by our parents and separated.

To me, it was nothing short of a miracle that now, here we were, all of us together. "Everybody get in close for a picture," my oldest sister said, taking charge again all these years later. *God has restored a family broken beyond hope,* I thought. For the first time I truly felt the depth of God's love and all its powerful possibilities. I wanted to help other people see that power in their own lives. I quit my detective job and became a pastoral counselor. I wanted to be where people's needs were immediate and raw.

On September 16, I got a call from a friend in San Jose. A Manhattan pastor, whose church was not too far from Ground Zero, was overwhelmed and needed help. Before dawn the next morning, I grabbed my bag and kissed my family good-bye. Traveling by air for the first time since the attacks, I was in for a shock. My police-style blue uniform and clerical collar got me plenty of attention. People just walked up to me and asked to pray with me in ticket lines, the restroom, at the baggage claim, anywhere their eyes caught mine. Even a security guard asked for my blessing while she pawed through my carry-on.

After landing in New York, I made my way down to the church. "You the chaplain from California?" a woman asked when I came in the door. I nodded. "Ready to talk to some firefighters?" "Sure," I said, expecting to walk right over to Ground Zero. "They're out on Staten Island," the woman said. "We'll take you over there in the van. Come on."

How strange it seemed to be heading away from Ground Zero after coming all this way, but I wound up at Homeport Naval Station, a staging area and recovery point for the Staten Island-based firefighters and relief workers going to and from the disaster site. "We've got infirmary units, showers, laptops, food and money," said the woman who welcomed me. "What we didn't have until now was God in the house."

I went over to a group of firefighters waiting to be called to Ground Zero. They were anxiously tapping their feet and fooling with their gear. I introduced myself and asked about a New York firefighter I'd worked side-by-side with in Oklahoma City, the leader of an elite squad. He was an inspiration then, and I hoped to run into him here.

"Have a seat, chaplain," one man said. The firefighter I'd asked about had rushed down in the first moments of the crisis to set up a command center at the base of the towers. He was lost in the collapse.

Speechless, I sat down on a pile of equipment. "We know, chaplain," another firefighter said. "Believe me, we know." So this is what it feels like. Everyone here has lost someone they care about.

One after another, the firefighters opened up and told me their stories. Grieving people don't want advice. They don't want sermons. They only want someone to listen to them. And that's what I did all night and into the morning. Then the firefighters got the call to go. "Chaplain, you coming with us?" I stood up. How could I say no after the conversation we'd just had?

Thirty minutes later our bus approached the smoldering ruins. We deployed three blocks away. The noise, the smell, the destruction—my senses were on overload. The tangled pile of debris rose more than 20 stories high in some places: Ground Zero. Smoke billowed up everywhere, as if issuing from Hell itself. The last survivor had been rescued less than 30 hours after the attack. No one had been found alive since. But of course we were all still hoping. Hope was a hard thing to let die.

I pulled on protective gear, and we walked through an entranceway cut into the mountainous pile, heading deep inside. The pile shifted constantly, rumbling as construction equipment passed. We had to step cautiously. Under our feet were voids—sections exposed when a beam was hoisted away. That's where we looked for signs of life, or death. We inched along, working with gloved hands, shovels, and picks. The temperature on the pile was close to 110 degrees, and our heavy gear was suffocating. For the duration of the 12-hour shift, I dug, I watched, I listened. I searched for my friend who was lost. No one was found alive.

The next day I went back to Ground Zero with the firefighters. We pulled another 12-hour shift. Again, our search was in vain. It was 2:00 A.M., rainy, foggy and cold. Yet the scene was eerily bright with giant Hollywood-style floodlights, so that workers in yellow slickers and huge machines could continue moving about on the pile, day or night, rain or shine. I was surrounded by people in utter anguish—a retired firefighter digging for his two sons, one a firefighter, the other a policeman; the detective who returned every day to the exact spot she was standing when everyone around her was crushed in the towers' collapse—tormented heroes who wondered why they lived and so many others died. In the midst of such despair, how could I give anyone hope?

You carried me through the collapse of my family, Lord. You healed me and called me to be a chaplain for a reason. But why? What use am I here? I passed up a ride back to Homeport on the police boat, instead opting to take the Staten Island ferry. I couldn't be with the other rescuers anymore that day, listen to any more outpourings of grief. I headed to the dock in Battery Park. It was misty, and a stiff wind blew in off New York Harbor. I turned up my coat collar. Were those footsteps? An elderly woman came up from the subway stairs. Beside her was a boy, dark-haired, maybe 11 years old. Both carried overstuffed black garbage bags on the verge of bursting. "Need help, ma'am?" I asked. "Where are you going?"

"To Staten Island," she said. I took the garbage bags. Maybe it was my clerical collar again, because the woman started talking. "My daughter is a drug addict, and tonight she kicked my grandson out of the house." The boy hung his head. A shiver ran down my spine. This night was never going to leave him, I knew. I reached out to put my arm around the boy while we walked. "My mother has lots of problems," he said. "And I don't know where my dad is."

My steps were slowed by the feeling that gripped me, that unmistakable sense of God's love I'd felt at my family reunion. I felt it again now, powerfully, in the midst of my own doubts. I felt him working through me to reach this one unhappy boy.

I told him a story about another boy, whose parents had abandoned him. "Do you know what he's doing now, all grown up?"

We'd stopped under a street lamp. The boy shook his head.

"Helping people at Ground Zero."

"Really?" he said. "At Ground Zero? How do you know?"

"Son, that boy was me."

He opened his eyes wide and they pooled with tears. Then I hugged him. "You'll cry a lot," I told him. "That's what I did. But remember, God brought me to you tonight. He loves you, never ever forget that. And He will keep sending people to help you if you just look for them wherever you go."

The boy slipped his hand in mine and we joined the grandmother on our way to the dock. I saw the arriving ferry, its lights burning bright through the mist. One person could make a difference. A little boy had just shown me how.[12]

The Way Out

BY RANDY FRANZ

*G*UAMA GOT SAVED TONIGHT!

It was one of the most triumphant moments in a 16-year effort by a tiny group of volunteer missionaries from Southern California called Christian Missionary Pilots. The 10-member traveling party rejoiced late into the night about Guama's decision and his salvation.

Guama was the baddest, meanest, most-feared, longest-term prisoner in Mexico's prison system. He killed fellow inmates . . . just for sport. He drank heavily and did lots of drugs. For nearly 40 years he had been in some of Mexico's worst prisons, with conditions that make an outhouse seem like an upgrade.

Now he was here, Maria Madre, an island 95 miles south of the Mexico port city of Mazatlan that serves as a rehabilitation prison, mostly for drug runners. There are no walls to keep the prisoners on the island. The armed guard on the beach, steep cliffs, and hungry sharks in the water do a pretty good job of that.

Prisoners live in small communities, some even with their families. A little "downtown" has been established with a small convenience store, a restaurant, even an outdoor cultural center. An elementary school and hospital were built about 10 years ago. Some inmates are given regular jobs, others sporadic assignments.

One of Guama's assignments 16 years ago was to cook for the Christian Missionary Pilots. It was CMP's first visit to the island. For the next four years, CMP made quarterly visits, and each time, Guama was their cook. He had mellowed a bit over time. No longer was he a callous murderer, although you probably wouldn't choose him to be your next-door neighbor. Guama watched the Americans closely. He listened to them. Over time, he began to converse with them and even developed a bit of a friendship. They prayed for Guama from the beginning.

The friendship grew stronger, and CMP members Hank Rowell and Gayle Cheatwood took turns telling Guama about Jesus Christ and the new life He offers. Each time they visited, Rowell and Cheatwood made sure to give Guama an opportunity to receive Christ, and each time Guama had a reason why he wouldn't. "I'm not ready," he would say. Still, they remained friends.

By the early 1990s, another inmate took over cooking chores for CMP's visits, but Guama always made a point to find the group to say hello. Rowell and Cheatwood wondered whether Guama would ever repent. They doubted it.

Then it happened. On November 8, 2001, CMP arrived with two dentists, a makeshift eye doctor, and a general physician who also was a pastor of a Christian church on the U.S. side of the border, at Yuma, Arizona. One other guest made the trip: *The JESUS film*, a cinematic portrayal of the life and message of Christ.

Rowell and Cheatwood showed the film on a Friday evening after working all day at the town's hospital. They set up a new DVD projector that Cheatwood had recently purchased, and let the movie roll in a small outdoor amphitheater. Afterward, the

Yuma pastor, Mario Avila, spoke in Spanish to the 25-30 people assembled and gave an altar call. Guama came forward.

"Jesus is not shoddy," Gauma told Avila. "He just talked regular."

Guama paused and looked straight into Avila's eyes.

"I'm ready."

Hours later, back at a bunkhouse where CMP stays, Cheatwood rejoiced in Guama's profession of faith.

"For years, we'd come down here and I'd go home blessed the most," says Bob Richardson, who piloted an old twin-engine Beechcraft 18 on the November 2001 trip. "This is medicinal, spiritually."

Why help Mexican criminals? It doesn't surprise Rowell that he receives such a question. The surprise is how it usually is phrased. Very negatively, as in, Why in the world would you want to help Mexican criminals?

"One guy refused to fly with me," says Rowell, CMP's president for 16 of the past 20 years. "He said, 'These guys are murderers, drug runners, molesters. Go help someone who deserves it.'"

Rowell's answer: "They [need] to hear the Gospel as much as anyone else."

What Rowell doesn't tell you is that he and CMP are the only Americans who go to the Islas Marias Federal Prison on Maria Madre. They also fly their own small, private planes at their own expense. A flight to the island with a six-seat, single-engine Cessna costs about $1,000 for fuel, landing fees, and maintenance costs.

"At one point, I was spending $30,000 a year," Rowell says. "My business was good, but now I'm retired. I can't do that."

CMP's volunteers—both pilots and non-pilots—also deliver food, medical supplies, multi-lingual Bibles and hymnals, and Christmas gifts to support other missionaries already operating in the United States and Mexico. They primarily focus on orphanages in Mexico and on U.S. Indian reservations in Arizona. Some of the missions are conducted by car or truck.

The Islas Marias trek struck a particular chord in Rowell back in 1985, when some Mexican doctors asked CMP to take them to the island after the devastating earthquake in Mexico City. Everything about the trip was difficult. For one, it was in a prison. And in that prison, the director (warden) cut outsiders little slack. Rowell and the doctors slept on cold, bare, concrete floors. They received scarce rations of water. "They treated us . . . like inmates," Rowell says.

Yet, as soon as he returned home to California, Rowell knew that he wanted to go back.

"That's my ministry," he told Bobbi. "I know it's hard. No one else wants to be there. No one else wants to go there. But I feel that I need to."

That was 16 years ago. Since then, Rowell has returned to Isla Maria every year, about four times per year. In addition to providing practical help such as dentistry and medical attention to the families, CMP gives gift bags filled with practical items such as new washcloths, toothbrushes, soap, etc. They also give away Bibles and witness to inmates and family members about Jesus Christ.

"Our purpose for being down there is to show them that God loves them," he says.

The directors who run the Islas Marias prison might last three years or three months before moving to another prison. Each director has his own priorities. One established farming to make the island self-sustaining. Others tried improving water supplies, making education a priority, improving medical facilities, or raising shrimp to generate revenue. Others simply flexed their dictatorial authority.

One year, the director was concerned about the expense of the food served to CMP. He wanted to keep track of the food charges and balance them against the medical work performed.

"In two days, we did $17,000 worth of dental work," says dentist Gayle Cheatwood, a 12-year veteran of Islas Marias trips. "The director decided not to charge us and it was never brought up again."

Two years ago, officials in Mexico City, who receive the authorizations for people to visit Islas Marias prison, wanted to honor CMP for its continued efforts. The people were amazed that they kept seeing this group's name on the sheet, year after year. Not even inmates' loved ones went with such regularity.

"Don't honor us," Rowell told the officials. "All I want is to keep the doors open and let us keep ministering."

The doors have not closed yet. Unless they do, Christian Missionary Pilots will continue to fly through them. "I love the freedom of being in the air," Rowell says as his 1975 Cessna 210 Centurion drifts out over the Gulf of Baja with a single engine propelling four adult passengers and gear. "Most of all, I love the fact that I can use this to go to people who need help. I'm not a doctor, but I can take doctors there. I'm not a dentist, but I can fly them there."[13]

Second Chance

BY JOHN W. KENNEDY

*T*HE DINNER TABLE at the Ron and Nora Cothran home is a picture of the idyllic family. The four good-looking children are polite, quiet, and respectful as Ron offers prayers of gratitude to the Lord. Afterward the children quote Scripture back and forth to each other. At bedtime, they hear Bible stories and pray.

This is a stable, peaceful home where the parents love the Lord and each other, where there is a clear delineation between right and wrong. Circumstances in the Cothran home in rural Nowata, Oklahoma, are in stark contrast to the environment these children encountered at birth. Then they were addicted to crack cocaine, sexually abused, neglected to the point of failing to thrive, and stunted by fetal alcohol syndrome. While heredity plays a role in such details as medical history, the Cothrans believe environmental conditions can strongly influence how a child turns out as an adult. They also believe that a child's outcome can be strongly influenced by God's redemptive love when those who are redeemed "Defend the poor and fatherless: [and] do justice to the afflicted and needy" (Psalm 82:3).

In her youth, Nora Cothran seemed an unlikely candidate to

become a godly and caring mother. She bore a child at age 16 and never married the father. Two years later, she married a 17-year-old high school dropout, but the marriage didn't last. Soon afterward, Nora had an emergency hysterectomy, ending any future childbirth plans. Ironically, the Cothrans' four adopted children have been born to mothers who have not only produced but relinquished multiple babies.

Ron and Nora met when they worked next to each other at a Tulsa envelope-making factory. They hung out together after work with other co-workers. Nora invited Ron on a date to a minor league baseball game—with her 8-year-old son, Allan. They began dating regularly, then moved in together.

Ron and Nora wanted more children. At the time, the state of Oklahoma required couples to be married in order to adopt. Ron and Nora planned on marrying anyway, and Ron formally adopted Allan after the 1990 wedding.

Meanwhile, Nora had been sending Allan to a Baptist church that had a bus ministry, just as her mother had done with her— before the teenage hormones took over. Allan attended Sunday morning, Sunday evening, and Wednesday evening services.

"I knew I wasn't living according to the Word of God—in fact, it was outright rebellion—but I wanted my son to go to church," Nora says.

Allan invited his mother and Ron to a choir performance at the church. Soon, Ron and Nora began attending church activities outside the church, such as a park cookout. "Nobody ever condemned us for not coming to church," Nora says. "They were kind, loving and nonjudgmental." After getting to know some of the families from church, the Cothrans began attending services.

"In church we found out what life should be like," Ron says. In

July 1992 they both professed Jesus as their Saviour.

Their newfound faith intensified the couple's desire to adopt children. Ron, who is white, and Nora, who is of Mexican and Cherokee/Choctaw Indian heritage, agreed to raise children of any race or physical condition. State officials told them they likely would have a long wait because they already had a child and many couples waiting to adopt had none. In a three-year span the Cothrans took care of 20 foster children.

But in 1997 they had an opportunity to adopt a sister and brother, Rees, 30 months, and Manny, 6 months. In 1999, they adopted Wyatt, 2 years and 10 months at the time.

The latest adoption, which happened in March 2002, came from an especially unusual series of circumstances. The birth mother had visited an abortion facility to schedule the procedure. She claimed not to know the father, with whom she had a one-night encounter. But just before the appointment, the woman discovered the money she had saved for the abortion had been stolen. The woman rescheduled, worked another three weeks to save enough money for the abortion and the same thing happened: stolen funds. The woman relayed her frustration to a co-worker, who attends a Bible-believing church in Bartlesville with the Cothrans. The co-worker told her she knew just the family who would want the baby, and a private adoption resulted. Although the Cothrans have had Liam since birth, earlier adoptions have been through the Oklahoma Department of Human Services after children were removed from homes. All the children are from Mexican and Native American heritage, as is Nora.

Even though the different children came to them addicted and violent, the Cothrans pray that God will help them equip the children with a practical appreciation of biblical truth and a love for their biological parents. They hope the children can someday find their biological parents and tell them about the hope and freedom they can have in the One who came to "heal the brokenhearted, to preach deliverance to the captives, and recovering of sight to the blind, to set at liberty them that are bruised" (Luke 4:18-19).

The Cothrans have been teaching church youth and speaking to youth groups for nearly a decade. Nora warns them not to make the same mistakes she did, not to abuse their bodies as she did. She believes the cancerous dysplasia on her cervix that caused the removal of her uterus was the result of being promiscuous so young. Nora says Joel 2:25—"I will restore to you the years that the locust hath eaten"—is one of her favorite Bible verses.

"God has restored the poor choices I had made that had been destructive," Nora says. "I had destroyed my ability to reproduce, but God made a way for me to have children."

Ron, now 37, still works in the envelope plant as a supervisor, but Nora, 39, believes her place is homeschooling the children. The couple has made the choice to put their energies into raising children, even if it means a simpler lifestyle. They hope to adopt 10 children eventually. Allan, now 22 and living in Bartlesville, wants to be a youth minister.

"Raising children is the best ministry I could ever hope for," Ron says. "The Lord has entrusted me with something very valuable. I wasted so many years living for myself. I want my kids to have a love for God that I didn't have for so long."[14]

The Best Inspirational Quotes

Being at peace with yourself is a direct result of
finding peace with God.
—Olin Miller

If you want to make an easy job seem mighty hard
just keep putting off doing it.
—Anonymous

Some people reach the top of the ladder of success
only to find it is leaning against the wrong wall.
—Anonymous

Tact is the art of making a point without making
an enemy.
—Dr. Jon Olson

It is impossible for that man to despair who
remembers that his Helper is omnipotent.
—Jeremy Taylor

Pray as if everything depended on God, and work as
if everything depended upon man.
—Cardinal Francis J. Spellman

Money is a very excellent servant, but a
terrible master.
—P. T. Barnum

Till Death Do Us Part

BY SUSAN G. HAUSER

*T*WO-YEAR-OLD KESTON Sakultarawattn is an inquisitive little boy. Cradled in his mother's arms, he loves inspecting the photos lining the hallway of his family's home in St. Helen's, Oregon. In a familiar ritual, Keston's mother, Haley, 26, carries him the length of the hallway, past the nursery where new baby sister Malee Sue is asleep, stopping at every photo until they reach the engagement portrait of his parents, Haley and Brian.

Keston points to Haley with happy recognition. But he's puzzled by the young man with almond eyes and dark hair. "Whozat?" he asks.

"That's Daddy," says Haley, "before he got hurt."

To Keston, Daddy is a man whose face is a patchwork quilt of leathery skin and who sits in a wheelchair, calls out to the son he can't see and embraces him with the remaining stumps of his arms. The boy never knew the face that smiles from the photo taken on December 18, 1995.

The young couple had been introduced three years earlier by Haley's sister, Angellee, who worked with Brian at his father's Thai restaurant. Angellee had a hunch that Brian's silly sense of humor would appeal to her younger sister, so she brought her to work one day. Haley was shy, worried that her adolescent acne would be a turnoff to the handsome, popular boy. But as their friendship grew, she began to feel beautiful in Brian's presence. He told her that true beauty derived from what was inside a person. Haley took the lesson to heart.

During that holiday season, the couple visited an uncle of Haley's who had lost both legs in a car accident. Afterward, they had one of the long, philosophical discussions they both relished. They talked about love, commitment and the insignificance of physical beauty compared with the ineffable beauty of the spirit. Brian affirmed that he would always be there for Haley, then asked, "Would you stick by me if I became disabled?" Haley replied without an instant's hesitation: "Of course." She had no inkling that she would soon find out if she had the courage of her convictions.

The day after Christmas, Brian, a forest-management trainee, was fixing some logging equipment at the tree farm owned by Angellee and her husband, Dan Kloppman. On bitterly cold days like this, Brian kept a fire burning in a metal barrel for warming his hands. The fire was too intense, so he grabbed a bucket of rainwater to throw on the flames.

The bucket, however, turned out to be filled with gasoline.

Angellee and Dan heard the explosion, followed by tortured screams. They sprinted down a forest trail and found Brian rolling on the ground, on fire from head to foot. Angellee screamed as Dan swatted frantically at Brian with his bare hands before remembering a blanket in the shed. But Brian's work clothes were so splattered with grease that even the blanket was no match for the flames at first. Still, Dan beat at the fire with the blanket until it was nearly out. Then he and Angellee ripped off Brian's boots and what remained of his smoldering clothes and lifted his charred and blistered body into their van.

Dan turned on the flashers and leaned on the horn as he sped toward the nearest hospital, just under 10 miles away. He held his own singed hand out the window to ease the pain. "Hang in there," he called to Brian in the back seat. Brian's throat was beginning to swell, making it difficult for him to breathe. But he managed to whisper; "I'm trying," before gasping, "If I die, tell Haley I love her."

Angellee called Brian's parents and Haley from the hospital. "Brian's been burned, and it's bad," she said, her voice quavering. When Haley and her mother, Brenda Havlik, arrived, Angellee related the story through racking sobs. Brian had already lost consciousness and was in a drug-induced coma to prevent shock. He lay in a nearby room on a stretcher, awaiting transfer by ambulance to the Oregon Burn Center at Legacy Emanuel Hospital in Portland, some 50 miles away.

Upon seeing her fiancé, who was covered to his neck with a blanket, Haley suppressed a cry of horror. His face was black and cinders dotted his mouth and teeth. His hair was singed and blood was caked on his neck and shoulders, where his skin had blistered. His whole body was swollen. Haley wanted to touch him, but was afraid she'd cause him further pain.

"Then a peace came over me," Haley recalls. "I didn't cry. I said, 'Brian, I love you. Everything will be okay. You're in God's hands.'"

At the Oregon Burn Center, Dr. Joseph Pulito's initial assessment was that Brian, who'd suffered third-degree burns over 95 percent of his body, had a minuscule chance of survival. Gently, the surgeon broke the news to Brian's mother, Jani, and father Chamrus "Mo" Sakultarawattn, a native of Thailand.

Jani begged Dr. Pulito to do whatever it took to save her son. "Brian is a devout Christian with a strong sense of purpose," she told him. "He would want to live, no matter what."

Over the objections of several of his colleagues, Dr. Pulito agreed to perform a risky, seven-hour surgery to remove Brian's dead skin and prepare his body for skin grafts. Privately, he doubted that his patient would survive long enough for the operation to happen. But after a few excruciating days of touch-and-go, Brian's condition had stabilized, and the grueling surgical process began.

Still deep in a drug-induced coma, Brian had all of his burned skin removed, and, in subsequent surgeries (22 over a seven-month period), replaced by donor skin and, eventually, grafts of his own skin harvested from his few unburned patches. Believing his vision to be intact, the doctors sewed his eyelids shut to keep the skin from contracting. Sadly, they were forced to amputate his left leg and right foot as well as both arms just above the elbow because impeded blood flow to his extremities had caused tissue death.

For weeks, Brian's body was wrapped, mummy-like, in head-to-toe bandages. The only indications that he was alive were the bleeps on the heart monitor and the repetitive whoosh of the ventilator. Throughout the entire ordeal, Brian's family stayed at his bedside and prayed for his recovery, as did their pastor and members of their tight-knit congregation. To his doctors' astonishment, Brian overcame one life-threatening crisis after another—a diseased bowel, blood disorders, and countless infections. Dr. Pulito's assisting resident, Kari Kramer, M.D., concluded that Brian's improbable survival was linked to the unceasing prayers of his loved ones. She became even more convinced after Brian escaped what appeared to be certain death from kidney failure. "I went home one night sure I would not see Brian alive again," she recalls. "The next morning, his kidneys had begun working for no evident medical reason. I truly felt I was witnessing a miracle."

Time and again, Dr. Pulito prepared the family for the worst. "I was constantly saying, 'This may be the beginning of the end,'" he recalls. "But every day, they'd say, 'He's still with us.' They were thrilled whenever he made it through another day."

In January 1996, after Brian had spent more than three weeks in a coma, doctors began to withdraw the powerful drugs that had shielded him from pain. Yet days went by with no physical response from him. An EEG indicated little or no brain activity. Desperate for some sign that he could hear them, Haley and Jani whispered, "Stick out your tongue, Brian." After what seemed an interminable wait, Brian's tongue poked through his lips. Haley and Jani, their eyes welling with tears, repeated the request. And again, Brian pushed out his tongue.

The women demanded another EEG; this time, it showed normal activity. When Ray Sakultarawattn arrived at the hospital that night expecting to bid his younger brother a final farewell, he found a scene of jubilant celebration. More joy erupted when Brian clearly mouthed the words "I love you" to Haley.

It would take two more months for Brian to be fully weaned off the ventilator. But after recovering consciousness, he quickly learned how to use the device that let him speak with the tracheotomy tube in his throat. He was in for the toughest conversations of his life. Feeling what doctors call "phantom pains" in his missing limbs, Brian, his eyes still sewn shut, asked his mother, "Were my hands burned really bad?" Jani had to break the painful news of the amputations.

As Brian struggled to absorb the full scope of his injuries, Haley said, "Brian, I love you very much."

"Why?" he shot back.

Haley was stunned by his acid tone, so uncharacteristic of the man she had known. Jani asked, "Brian, if this had happened to Haley instead of you, would you still love her?"

"Yeah," he answered quietly.

Brian cried for a while, mourning his lost limbs—the nimble legs and feet that had taken him on long mountain hikes, the muscular arms and hands that had been so adept at construction work. Most of all, he mourned the feel of Haley's hand in his and the pleasure of wrapping his arms around her petite body.

But a flicker of his trademark impish humor soon peeked through. "Guess this means you won't have to buy me a wedding ring," he teased Haley.

"Yes, I will," she said. "And you're going to wear it around your neck!"

But one more agonizing loss would follow. The doctors had been confident that Brian's vision would return once the effects of the coma drugs wore off. But a week after regaining consciousness and having his bandages and stitches removed (a procedure that gave Jani and Haley their first glimpses of a face that looked, in Jani's words, "like a skeleton, not a person"), Brian still could not see. When the ophthalmologist shone a bright light directly in his eyes, he had no reaction.

Dr. Pulito theorized that the intense swelling and tissue damage from the burns had kept blood from reaching Brian's retinas, most likely causing blindness within 48 hours of his accident. Early tests had shown Brian's retinas to be pale, but the ophthalmologist had attributed this condition to the young man's Asian heritage. Now it was apparent that the paleness had been a function of blocked blood flow.

Everyone, including all of Brian's caregivers, was devastated. Throughout his ordeal, the young man had held on to the promise of his restored sight, of his happiness at once again seeing Haley and his family. Now, as he contemplated permanent darkness, the brave young man's spirits reached a new low. He lay in bed and wept bitterly. When Haley phoned her parents with the bad news, she was crying so hard no words came.

As profound and pervasive as Haley's grief was, nothing—not the horrible scarring of Brian's face, or the amputations, nor his blindness—could shake her fierce commitment to her fiancé. She was constantly at his side. Indeed, one of the few times she left the hospital was to attend a bridal show to pick out her wedding dress.

Observing Haley's unswerving devotion, Dr. Pulito worried that the 19-year-old had painted herself into a corner. He wondered if she fully grasped the enormity of Brian's handicaps and their effect on the life they had envisioned. Perhaps all she needed was some-one's loving permission to break off the engagement. The doctor confided his concerns to Jani.

"We wouldn't have thought less of Haley if she'd made that deci-sion," says Jani. "But her position was very clear. She told me once, 'I don't care what Brian can or can't do. I just want to be able to talk to him.' But I did tell her mom, 'If Haley decides she can't deal with this, we'll understand.'"

"I told Jani that it wasn't just Haley who was in love with Brian—her dad and I were, too," says Brenda. "It would have ripped us apart to just suddenly turn him loose."

Brian still wanted to get married, but he, too, worried that Haley had been put in an impossible position. Yet he also understood that her willingness to sacrifice was part of who she was—and what he loved about her. "We believe that love isn't something you turn on and off when it's convenient," he says. "It is a decision, not just a feeling."

So he asked her, "Are you sure you want to get married?"

"Yes," she said, without hesitation.

After seven months in the hospital, Brian came home. The wedding was still on—with Dr. Pulito's blessing. "Brian is a lucky man," he says. "He has someone who loves him for him." The fact that Brian's ability to father children was intact meant that the couple could have the family they'd always planned. "A dad is there for love and support," says Dr. Pulito. "Brian can do that."

The couple married on November 1, 1997. Brian's father, his best man, placed the wedding ring on Haley's finger; she slipped a chain holding Brian's ring around his neck. As Brian, wearing leg prostheses beneath his tux and guided by Haley's hand on his upper arm, walked down the aisle with his bride, radiant in white taffeta, many of the 450 guests sobbed quietly. Suddenly, Haley's brother Rusty and two of her uncles burst into a silly song—"Loving You Lots and Lots," from the movie *That Thing You Do!* The tension was broken and guests began laughing through their tears.

The couple's first home was an apartment attached to his parents' house. With the occasional help of visiting nurses, Haley became Brian's primary caregiver. Besides bathing and feeding him, she learned to cleanse his wounds, change his dressings and help with his daily stretching exercises.

Before the accident, Brian and Haley had dreamt of living a simple life that included frequent hikes and camping trips. Brian had already begun building a log cabin where the young couple planned to live. "I thought my life was all planned out," Brian says. "While my body was burning, I remember thinking, *Guess I was wrong.*"

During Brian's long stay in the hospital, a local newspaper ran an article about the couple, which mentioned that Brian had poured the foundation for a cabin he would now never finish. Deeply moved by Brian's story, Lori Albert, a firefighter in St. Helen's, decided to enlist the services of her fellow volunteers in building the house. Eventually, hundreds of people from the community contributed money, materials and labor to the project that Albert dubbed "Brian's House: a Foundation of Faith."

Two years later, the "cabin" (which had morphed into a 2,200-square-foot house) was ready, fully customized for Brian's needs: A battery-powered lift carries him in a sling from the master bedroom to the bathroom with its roll-in shower. Another room holds exercise equipment. In a sling, Brian bounces on a trampoline for cardio exercise and does crunches and leg lifts. He also goes to a local gym with a caregiver several times a week to work on strengthening machines.

The couple soon fell into a comfortable routine of church activities, entertaining and gardening. Brian, who had worked as a cook at his father's restaurant, provides tips as Haley prepares the meals that she feeds him. For diversion, he listens to music or books on tape, and in the summer they drive to campgrounds where they stay in a tent and Brian fishes, courtesy of a contraption that lets him activate an electric reel with the end of his arm.

Brian's ability to maintain a positive outlook and to avoid bitterness and depression is a near-miracle. Haley, however, acknowledges that she has down days, when the "if onlys" flood her mind. "I sometimes wonder, *What if I had chosen differently?*" she admits. "I'll see married couples, and I'll miss all the stuff we used to do, like hiking. I'll think of where I could be or all the fun I could be having. But I also think, *How would I feel if I'd left him?* Besides, I already knew that Brian was who God had chosen for me, and what happened didn't change that. He's still Brian."

Her greatest sorrow, she says, is that he can't see. So she

describes herself to him, detailing her outfits and changes in her hairstyle. She paints a verbal picture of the world around them—the landscapes changing with the seasons, the growth of their garden and even new models of cars. In return, Brian lightens her days with his irreverent humor. "Can you help me out?" he'll ask her. "I'm a little short-handed."

His humor is a tonic, but nothing has revitalized Haley as much as becoming a mother. The moment Keston, born on August 22, 2001, was placed in her arms, Haley felt as if her husband had been reborn. In her son's face she sees the same almond eyes, dark hair and soft skin that she remembers in Brian.

In autumn 2002, the couple had another scare: Brian's kidneys suddenly failed. He began dialysis but needed a kidney transplant to survive. Luckily, his sister, Linda Mitts, was a perfect match. That November, she donated a kidney to her little brother.

The procedure (Brian's 43rd surgery since the accident) was a success for both siblings. Once again, Brian's indomitable spirit had vanquished a grave threat to his life. A year and a half later, he remains healthy and pain free, taking only anti-rejection drugs for the transplant. Last summer, the couple had more good news: the birth of their daughter, Malee Sue.

Brian and Haley feel they have immeasurable riches to share with their children—a wealth of wisdom that was forged in a fire. "We will encourage Keston and Malee to be grateful, to not take things for granted," says Brian. "We want them to keep what's important always in focus."

The most profound lessons, of course, will require no words. The sheer example of the couple's life together will teach their children all they'll ever need to know about faith, commitment and the power of love.[15]

Blessing in Reverse

BY KATHE CAMPBELL

*H*ER CHILDREN AND GRANDCHILDREN rolled her into the day room just before the Super Bowl party commenced. She appeared puzzled over all the fuss as she slumped awkwardly in her wheelchair.

The hospital staff and volunteers had prepared a delectable table. Melons, meats, and salads, along with punch and a fancy football cake for all patients and guests in the transitional area to enjoy.

My husband, Ken, had asked me to come early for the party that day. He was recovering from complications as a result of an elk careening through his windshield last fall. Our daughter, Molly, and her husband had also joined the festivities to help celebrate Pop's 75th birthday. We ate like gluttons that afternoon, the party cuisine far superior to the usual hospital fare.

Suddenly I noted the lady in the wheelchair was quite alone. She had no party snacks and it appeared her family had left her high and dry. The nurse confirmed my suspicions, stating they had little patience with their mother's stroke and had left. My jaw dropped. "Those big kids should be spanked," I blurted out with disdain!

Ken had found an interesting fellow to talk gold-panning with,

so I pulled a chair out at the lady's table and boldly sat down.
Her stroke had rendered her quite helpless. Her head drooped
down on her chest, and her right arm hung limp at the side of her
wheelchair. She seemed incapable of uttering even a grunt while
knots and snarls sadly bedecked her tousled hair. I introduced
myself as Ken's wife and asked if she would care for a plate of food.
She nodded despairingly as her surprised and tearful eyes met
mine. I longed to hug her tight while secretly pondering her fate.

It was difficult stifling my feelings of disgust with this woman's
family, but I swallowed hard and attempted communications with
Pauline. I tied a cowboy kerchief-style towel about her neck, placed
her plate on the table, and she dove in, picking up each morsel with
her left hand like a baby in a highchair. She was even able to lift
her cup of lemonade emitting a big "ahhh" after each sip. Pauline
was having a good afternoon.

I asked the nurse concerning Pauline's rag-tag hairdo and she
brought a cup of water, some snarl-eze and a small brush. Just why
no one had seen to this dear lady's coiffure was an inhumane mystery to me. Molly and I took turns combing and brushing the tan-
gles ever so carefully until her hair was damp, shiny, and free of
snarls. While patting her head gently with a towel and scrunching
strands with our fingers, her old perm began to take shape. What a
joyous sight watching Pauline peering gleefully into a hand mirror
as though she was ready for a prom.

I again sat beside her, slowly enunciating about grandkids and
helping her with her cake. Suddenly she grabbed at my right arm
and began a series of tugs and frowns. It didn't take an Einstein to
realize she had become aware of my "conversation piece."

With a big grin, I raised my right hook onto the table just as she
let out a wail. Thankfully football was so loud on the big screen,

barely a soul paid mind to the commotion. I insisted I was fine, that it was an old injury and the hook worked better than my good arm anyway. She looked devastated, so I hugged her again and whispered in her ear to please not feel badly for me. While adeptly demonstrating my prosthetic contraption, pure amazement flooded over her face, and she slowly began to smile while the last of her tears tumbled off her cheeks.

"Dear God in heaven," I mused, "this dear soul, in all of her physical frustrations and mental anguish, feels an abiding love and compassion for me in spite of herself."

Who makes people like this? Are they born this way? God, in his infinite wisdom, didn't play favorites. He lovingly created hearts of gold in the lame, the wretched, and the downtrodden believers of the world.

This had truly been a blessing in reverse, and I thank my lucky stars I was afforded the opportunity to meet this gracious and loving human being. May God be with her 'til we meet again.[16]

This House Saved My Son's Life

BY ANNE CASSIDY

*D*URING HER SECOND PREGNANCY, Renee Yoder of Bristol, Indiana, knew something was wrong. "My first baby kicked like a soccer player," she says. "This time I could feel movement, but nothing like it should be." The ultrasound and amniocentesis showed no problem, but when Justin was born in May 1996, he had big blue eyes, a full head of blond hair—and spina bifida, a birth defect of the spinal column that causes paralysis of the legs and loss of bladder and bowel control. Justin was rushed from the small local hospital where he was born to a larger one in South Bend, where he had emergency surgery.

As the days passed, Justin had difficulty swallowing and breathing, and he was additionally diagnosed with Arnold-Chiari syndrome, a brain malformation. Doctors inserted a shunt in his brain to drain off excess fluid caused by the malformation and hooked him up to a respirator so he could breathe. Not until he was moved from his incubator to an ambulance that would transport him to Riley Children's Hospital in Indianapolis—three hours away—was Renee allowed to hold her son for the first time, and it was just for a few seconds. Doctors said he might not survive the trip.

Renee and her husband, Mike, both 38, were familiar with children's health problems. Their older son, Colten, was born with retinitis pigmentosa, a hereditary condition that causes degeneration of the retina and eventual severe vision loss. But with their younger son, his very life hung in the balance. The Yoders left 3-year-old Colten with relatives and rushed to Indianapolis. Justin survived the trip, but his parents were told he was in for a long hospital stay. So Mike and Renee arranged to move into the Ronald McDonald House in Indianapolis. Mike, a long-haul truck driver who was paid by the mile, had to keep working to pay the bills. Renee spent every waking minute with her newborn son. "I held him whenever I could, because I never knew what would happen next," she says.

And a lot did happen. "After 9 P.M. there were no phone calls allowed into the Ronald McDonald house unless it was an emergency, so every time the phone rang after 9 P.M., the hair on the back of my neck would stand up because I knew it was bad news for somebody," Renee says. "Five or six of those times the call was for me." There were emergency surgeries and blood transfusions, but somehow, Justin hung on.

Eight months and several corrective surgeries later, the immediate danger had passed, and the Yoders brought Justin home. Still, his prognosis was far from promising: He still couldn't breathe or eat on his own. He would need round-the-clock care and a ventilator. Medicaid allowed for some home nursing, but Justin's case was complicated; often the nurse and Renee were learning together. "It took me six months not to jump out of my skin every time an alarm went off," Renee says. "We didn't know whether it was a problem with a machine or with Justin." Because Justin had an impaired breathe-swallow-gag reflex he often developed pneumonia. Renee kept their packed bags by the door because she never knew when she'd need to rush Justin to the hospital.

The Yoders' dilapidated two-bedroom house in Elkhart, which they were renting with the intention to eventually buy, wasn't helping matters. Justin had to stay in the living room because it was the only room large enough to contain all his equipment, and there were always wind gusts from the door opening and closing. "The house was drafty and old," Mike says. "There was a lot of moisture, so there were molds. There were rotten sub floors and three layers of carpet. Everything was dank and musty." Adds Renee: "The house was pretty much falling down around us."

Renee tried to go back to the waitressing job she'd held for years, but after rushing home twice in one day to find the ambulance at her house because Justin had stopped breathing, she realized her sons needed her full time. The family's livelihood depended on Mike being out on the road, usually for weeks at a time. Before Justin was born, the family was making do financially, but now they were behind on bills. It was a frightening, exhausting time for everyone.

Then, in the spring of 1998, Renee saw a story about a Habitat partner family on the local news. She stopped by the Elkhart County Habitat for Humanity office, in Goshen, and learned that it was the last day to get an application. The couple rushed around like crazy getting the personal recommendations and other paperwork required. It was April 18, Mike's birthday, when they submitted their forms. The family's luck was about to change.

Elkhart County's executive director, Chris Lehman, was looking for families who could pay back a zero-interest mortgage and a $300 down payment on a $78,700 house and be willing to help others build their homes. The Yoders looked like good bets. Most importantly, "A family must demonstrate need, " Lehman says. "And that was no problem with the Yoders either." Mike and Renee met with various Habitat board members, trying to contain their enthusiasm as each meeting brought them closer to their own home. At the last one, the whole family was there, "and we were pathetic looking," Renee says with a laugh. "Justin was on life support, and Colten had just had an operation so he was bandaged. I guess they saw our need, alright." A few days later, when some board members stopped by to give the Yoders the good news, the family wasn't home: Justin had pneumonia and they had rushed him to Riley Hospital in Indianapolis—again.

When they did receive the news a few days later, the Yoders were thrilled. "I come from a poor family," says Renee. "No one ever had a brand-new home before." To fulfill Habitat's sweat-equity requirement, the Yoders went to work helping others build their houses. Mike squeezed in hours whenever he could. And when the nurse came to relieve Renee, she'd put in her hours, too. With continued health emergencies for the children to be dealt with, it took almost two years before ground was broken for the Yoders' house.

Meanwhile, Chris Lehman and his volunteers were figuring out how Habitat could best help the family. "The Yoders' house was basically all about Justin," Lehman explains. It would have to be almost 500 square feet larger than the standard 1,040-square-foot three-bedroom model to give Justin a bathroom and bedroom large enough to accommodate his equipment. Doors and halls needed to be wider to allow for his wheelchair. Justin's room got a walk-in closet to hold his equipment, medications and oxygen tanks. The room itself could easily contain a hospital bed, wheelchair and ventilator—as well as his toys.

While the other two bedrooms would have carpeting, Justin's

room and the rest of the house would have vinyl flooring to keep dust to a minimum and allow for him to get around more easily. A donated air filter would remove impurities from the air. Volunteers would also have to construct a concrete ramp, so Lehman teamed up with a local company that, in turn, donated the railings. One of the most ingenious devices in the Yoders' house is the auxiliary generator. Lehman contacted the local gas company and explained that the family needed some sort of backup generator for Justin's life-support equipment. The company donated a natural gas-powered generator with internal sensors that detect in an instant when electricity has failed and automatically turns itself on. "That was a $15,000 gift," Lehman says. "It took the whole community to make this house happen."

But there was one more major hurdle, and this time it wasn't one of the boys, but Renee herself who was in trouble. Shortly after the Yoders were picked to be a Habitat family, Renee's mother, then just 58, died from complications due to surgery for a brain aneurysm. Aneurysms tend to run in families, and Renee soon learned that the same condition had killed her grandmother. One of Justin's nurses, who'd become a friend, urged Renee to have an MRI scan. But with no insurance, she had no way to pay for the test. Once church friends learned of her need they raised $2,300 for Renee to have the MRI—and it showed a 9 mm aneurysm behind her left eye. Repairing it would require complicated surgery that Renee feared would leave her blind or even more of an invalid than her son.

The house still wasn't finished; there was almost a month's worth of work to do. But Renee had two young sons to care for and a time bomb in her skull. "There was a danger of the aneurysm bursting," says Mike, "so it was the lesser of two evils to have the surgery done." Renee realized that she had no choice. (Medicaid paid for the surgery.)

Not only did Renee come through the surgery with flying colors, but for the few weeks she was in the hospital and recuperating, Habitat volunteers, spurred on by her brother, Jesse Clair, went into overdrive so the Yoders could finally move into their new home in June 2000. "There's nothing I can ever do to thank my brother and the volunteers for working their tails off before I got home," Renee says. Mike thinks of the volunteers as guardian angels: "We were well watched over because a lot of people took it upon themselves to help us."

It's been almost three years since the Yoders moved in and the family has been transformed. Colten has acres of land to romp around, and Justin has entered kindergarten. The family's circular driveway allows the school bus to pull up to the door and pick him up.

But of all the miracles wrought by the Yoders' new home, the most amazing one is this: Since moving into the house, Justin's health has improved. "The best thing ever to happen to him was this house," says Renee. Justin now needs the ventilator only when he sleeps.

Sometimes, when Renee and Mike think about everything that's happened to them during the last seven years, it takes their breath away. "I was pretty cynical before Justin came along, but this whole thing has restored my faith in humanity," Mike says. As for Renee, one day when the family was all moved in and settled, she went out into the field in front of their new house. "I put my head on my knees and just thanked God that everything was okay. I thought about how awesome it all was, and how we were so truly blessed."[17]

The Best Inspirational Quotes

The trouble with stretching the truth is that it's apt to snap back.

—Anonymous

He who provides for this life, but takes no care for eternity, is wise for a moment, but a fool forever.

—Tillotson

A coincidence is a small miracle where God prefers to remain anonymous.

—Anonymous

Sometimes the Lord calms the storm; sometimes He lets the storm rage and calms His child.

—Anonymous

The teacher asked the pupils to tell the meaning of loving-kindness. A little boy jumped up and said, "Well, if I was hungry and someone gave me a piece of bread that would be kindness. But if they put a little jam on it, that would be loving-kindness."

—Anonymous

Consider the turtle. He makes progress only when he sticks his neck out.

—Anonymous

Life and Death on Palos Verdes Lake

BY LARRY HICKS

*Y*OU KNOW THOSE RECRUITING ads for the
Marines that you see on TV? Those pictures of ready-for-any-
thing guys who seem fit for whatever comes their way? Well, that
was me. For 22 years I was the quintessential U.S. Marine. I was a
bodybuilder—210 pounds of raw muscle—still able to bench
press 425 pounds at age 50.

Now I couldn't even bring myself to look at the weights at my
gym. The sight of them was like a cruel taunt. Two years earlier I
got head and neck cancer. I beat it, but chemotherapy and surgery
shrank me to 140 pounds. A few months after I got out of the hospital, I lay on my back on the weight bench, planted my feet on the
floor, and tried to raise the empty barbell off the weight track.
Only 35 pounds, but I could not do it. *I'm no longer a man*, I
thought.

One thing was certain. My Marine days were over. My wife,
Donna, and I bought a house on Palos Verdes Lake, a remote spot
in southeaster Alabama. We moved there because we love to fish—
out back there's a 14-foot boat tied to our dock, ready to go—and
also because I thought the peaceful lake would calm me. But it did-
n't. "You're in remission now," my doctor had told me. "However, I'm

sorry to say, the cancer will likely return."

One spring evening not long after the doctor's prognosis, I slumped on the living room couch beside my wife, watching the sunset. Staring out across the peaceful lake was about the only thing that gave me pleasure anymore. *How many more do I have left?* I couldn't help wondering.

"Honey? Do you hear that?" Donna asked. I sat straight up, my old Marine instincts kicking in. It sounded like a loud, sputtering engine.

Donna got up and peered out the glass door overlooking the lake. "Larry, look how low that plane is flying!" A small, twin-engine aircraft swooped just above the treetops. *My gosh,* I thought, *he can't know that two sets of power lines cross the lake.*

I saw the pilot barely clear one set of lines, then bank low. He probably thinks he's safe. An instant later, he smashed into the second set. The plane flipped and crashed upside down into the lake.

"Call 911!" I yelled to Donna and took off down the steps to the dock and my fishing boat. The plane was about 100 yards offshore, already almost completely submerged in about eight feet of water. Some of the fuselage and part of one wing jutted above the surface. *Where is the pilot?*

I flicked on the boat engine and headed toward the wreckage. The light was fading fast. Help was still precious minutes away. Suddenly it hit me. I was the only one who could save the pilot. But could I, in my condition? Could I dive into the water, find the pilot and pull him back to the surface? *Lord,* I prayed, *I can't even lift thirty-five pounds.* I cut the motor. Black smoke rose from one of the plane's engines. My eyes stung, and the acrid stench burned my lungs. Pools of high-octane fuel fanned across the rippling water. *The plane's going to explode!*

In the Marines we'd trained for this type of emergency. I had to locate the pilot, get him out of the plane and to the surface, check his breathing, stop his bleeding, treat him for shock. I knew that I had just minutes to save him. I roped the boat to the fuselage, stripped off my shoes and shirt, took a deep breath and dove.

I could barely see through the fog of engine fuel and oil. I followed the contour of the aircraft with my hands. I thrust them into every opening I came across, searching for the cockpit. Already my lungs were about to burst. Suddenly I felt the outline of a seat. Empty. I kicked to the surface. *He has to be in there.*

I gulped some air and dove. *Where is the pilot?* Feeling my way along the lake bottom, I circled the plane again. *I'm not giving up,* I thought. *Not on him, not on me.* My lungs screamed for air. I forced myself to stay submerged, to keep searching. Nothing. I had to get another breath. I reached down to push off from the fuselage. My hand swept across something. The pilot. The crash had thrown his seat into the nose of the plan. He was upside down in his rigging. *Get him out of there,* I told myself. I fumbled with his seat belt. My mind was getting foggy. *Hang on, buddy, I'm coming back.* I shot to the surface, sucked in more air, dove back down.

My fingers felt something cold and hard. The seat belt release. I gave it a push. The pilot was free for me to pull from the cockpit. I wrapped my arms around him and tugged hard. No use. He felt like a sack of wet cement. My lungs were giving out again. *I need you, Lord.* I pulled again with all my might. Suddenly the pilot and I floated to the surface.

I paddled us to the fuselage and grabbed it with my left hand. I looked at the pilot. He wasn't breathing. *A great pair we make,* I thought. *One of us sick, the other drowning.*

I turned him around, gripped my right arm around his rib cage and squeezed as hard as I could. Water shot from his mouth. But it didn't get him breathing.

I wedged him against the wing with my body, cradled his head in my right arm and blew into his mouth. Once. Twice. My own lungs—weakened by cancer and chemotherapy—were raw from the acrid fumes. *I don't know if I can save him,* I thought. *I can barely breathe.* His face was sickly white, his lips blue. I tried a third time, and a fourth. *Lord, how much time do I have? Help me.* I tried once more.

His chest moved. He gave a shallow, strangled cough. Blood seeped from his mouth. He was still unconscious, but at least he was breathing again. Pretty banged up, though, particularly around the head and neck. *I can't risk lifting him into the boat.* How long could I keep us above water? I felt weaker by the second. *Where is the rescue squad? Lord, there's only you.*

All at once I knew we were going to be all right, I was going to be all right, no matter what. A greater strength was supporting us. "Don't you worry, we're going to make it," I said to the pilot. I didn't even know if he could hear me, but I just had to hear myself say it.

A voice came across the water. "Larry, we're coming!" A boat cut through the haze. Seconds later we were pulled to safety.

EMTs stabilized the pilot and whisked him off in an ambulance. Others worked on me. My body had taken a beating—first- and second-degree burns over 50 percent of my neck, chest and stomach. My lungs were singed. I'd torn a ligament in my finger gripping the plane.

On the way to the hospital I asked about the pilot. "His left leg is shattered, he broke some ribs and probably has a collapsed lung," one EMT said. "But he'll make it, thanks to you."

Another EMT interrupted. "Buddy, do you know who you

saved? That's Jack Roush, the NASCAR team owner. Mark Martin and Matt Kenseth drive for him. In the racing world, he's as big as they get."

It occurred to me that I saved someone else pretty important too—myself.

The next day the newspapers called me a hero. But that kind of talk really didn't matter to me. What counted was that for so long, I'd been depressed—even ashamed—over the things I could no longer do. *I'm ready, Lord,* I thought. *If the cancer comes back, with your help I'll fight it.*

The first day I could, I headed straight to the gym, eager to get back to the weight bench, ready again for whatever came my way.[18]

One Friendship at a Time

BY BERT GHEZZI

WHEN ASSOCIATE PASTOR, Paul Miller, first became a Kids Hope USA mentor to a child named Simon, the boy was in such frequent fights that he had a nearly permanent place in the principal's office. Simon's life has begun to change in the two-and-a-half years that he's met with Miller, pastor of Covenant Life Church in Grand Haven, Michigan.

"Sometimes we go over his homework, sometimes we play games or read books. Mostly we just talk," Miller says. "The principal told me that Simon has done a complete about-face in his respect for his peers, for authority, and for himself. All I do is show up each week. I believe in him and pay attention to him. Every week we end our time together the same way: I tell Simon he is a good kid, and he tells me he will do his best. I am amazed how God uses that hour in such big ways."

When Virgil Gulker developed Kids Hope to help at-risk children in public schools, he asked police, teachers, clergy, and social workers what the church could do for at-risk kids, many of whom live in impoverished and single-parent households. The resounding answer: What children need most is a stable relationship with a caring adult.

Gulker started Kids Hope in 1995 with three churches and schools in southwestern Michigan. Today 217 programs in 27 states provide mentors to about 3,800 children. Gulker connects a church with a neighboring elementary school, and church members become one-on-one mentors to at-risk students. A mentor spends one hour a week with a child—tutoring, helping with homework, playing, or just visiting. But the underlying purpose of the hour is to create a friendship with an adult that brings consistency to a child's life.

Mentoring relationships transform children. Consider Annie, a student in Baton Rouge, Louisiana, who has five family members in prison. When school began last year, Annie was withdrawn, and doing very little school work. After four months with a mentor, she is performing above the class average in all subjects.

"Principals tell us that between 98 and 100 percent of students in these adult-child relationships show significant improvement in academic performance and attitude," Gulker says.

A consistent and nurturing relationship with a mentor fosters a child's ability to learn. "Research shows that children in unstable environments are left with two physiological responses: fight or flight," says Joseph Loconte, a fellow of the Heritage Foundation. "Only emotional stability allows brain function to improve and learning to take place."

Educators such as Carmen Hannah, principal of Van Raalte Elementary School in Holland, Michigan, say that mentoring also helps children stop bad behavior. Says Hannah, whose school has the largest Kids Hope program in the nation: "The pride our students show in their work and their increased motivation for learning gives them so much confidence that they no longer need to fool around or be belligerent to get their need for attention fulfilled."

Gulker likes to tell the story of Jason, a five-year-old kinder-gartener who had been arrested 25 times for arson. Jason had attended a correctional school for pyromaniacs, but he continued to set fires. "The boy is just searching for proof that someone cares about him," said the principal at the correctional school. A year later the principal and the pastor of the church offering Kids Hope at his school invited Gulker to speak to other local principals. He opened by asking about the young arsonist.

"That child is in our Kids Hope program," said the principal.

"What?" asked the pastor, "Who in my church is working with him?"

"You are," said the principal, "and you have changed his life."

Not knowing the worst about the boy he befriended, the mentor had expected the best and got it. Jason is now a well-adjusted member of his class and an excellent student.

Kids Hope's strongest champions are principals and teachers who see how it offers a fresh start to disadvantaged children. Thirteen principals in Terre Haute, Indiana, recently asked 150 pastors to provide mentors for their schools.

Educators say the program builds faithfulness and stability among mentors and students. "My children face abandonment issues constantly," says Glenda O'Banion, a school principal in Hammond, Louisiana, "and they've been abandoned by people who said, 'We care.' I'm an old lady, and I've been in education for 30 years. This is the first program I've seen carry through on all the principles they first stated they would do. I've never seen anything like this." She wants mentors for 300 of the 412 poor kids in her school.

"We're not interested in good intentions," Gulker says. "We put extraordinary emphasis on the commitment the church needs to make to the child."

While participants in the program are required to respect the school administrators' obligation to enforce church-state separation, they are not prevented from sharing their faith with children and their families. With parents' permission, a mentor may invite a child to events and activities at the church. A mentor who shows the love of Christ at the school is free to speak about God at church. Kids Hope directors advise school administrators that evangelism may occur in church settings.

The church designates a behind-the-scenes prayer partner for each mentor-child relationship. "While prayer is not allowed in public schools," says Gulker, "Kids Hope has 3,800 prayer partners infusing schools with prayer each week."

Churches are discovering that caring for kids opens the way for reaching their parents and siblings. Consider the spiritual impact on Colton, a six-year-old first-grader, and Susan, his mom. The boy had been abused by a disappearing dad and suffered with Attention Deficit Disorder. Calvin Christian Reformed Church in Holland, Michigan, paired Colton with Herk Bos, a retired man. The relationship affected both of their lives, but after five years, Bos died. Now in seventh grade, Colton wrote this memorial to honor him:

Mr. Bos was not only my mentor but also my best friend! Some of my favorite memories are when we visited his childhood farm so he could show me where he fished as a child. He taught me how to fillet a fish, set a swivel hook, and how to bait a crawfish. . . . He taught me to be a master gardener but most importantly to love and trust in the LORD with all my heart!

Herk Bos's care persuaded Susan, Colton's mother, to accept

Christ and to join the church. Recently she helped establish a Bible study that attracts a dozen Kids Hope moms to church every Wednesday.

"Despite compelling evidence that most people accept Christ by age 18," says Gulker, "many churches continue to put the bulk of their efforts in programs for people 20 or older. But by reaching at-risk children, Kids Hope gives churches a proven strategy and a relational platform to reach their neighbors in the name of Christ."[19]

Finding Purpose in Pain

BY CORRIE CUTRER

LOVE NOTE IS STILL visible on Evelyn Husband's makeup mirror in her bathroom. The words were written with a bar of soap by her husband, astronaut Rick Husband, shortly before his departure as commander of the space shuttle *Columbia* on January 16, 2003. It reads, "I love you Evey, love Rick." It was only meant to appear there temporarily.

"Of course I can't wash that off," Evelyn says.

It's been [more than] a year since Evelyn stood with the other families of the space shuttle *Columbia's* crew at the landing site in Cape Canaveral, Florida, waiting for her husband to return home. The shuttle was just minutes from landing when NASA's Missions Control lost contact with the *Columbia* crew. The next few moments were a blur of events: video images of *Columbia* breaking apart over the Texas skyline, NASA officials scrambling to move the family members away from view of television cameras. Evelyn remembers looking at the faces of her son, Matthew, and daughter, Laura, then 7 and 12. Matthew turned to his mother. "He said, 'I guess I'm not going to be in Indian Guides with Dad at the YMCA anymore.' It was the first thing that hit him," Evelyn says.

Laura also was trying to process this new gap in her life. "Who's going to walk me down the aisle one day, Mamma?" she asked, teary-eyed. "Who's going to help me with my math homework?"

"They were instantly aware we were a different unit," Evelyn, 45, says of her children.

So began the Husbands' painful journey of loss. In the months following the accident, Evelyn, a committed Christian, spoke openly about how the faith she found as a 13-year-old girl had sustained her. Two days after the accident, she appeared on the Today show and shared how she was trusting in God to give her strength through this difficult time. As Evelyn recited the words of Proverbs 3:5-6, the show's producers flashed the verses on the screen.

That was the beginning of Evelyn's efforts to deliver a powerful message: Even in the midst of intense suffering, God is faithful. In recent months, she's told her story to tens of thousands of women across the country at Women of Faith conferences.

"Most of you aren't going to lose the person you love most on national television," she told an audience of women in California last summer. "But every person will face big tragedies and little everyday crises. Your only consistency is Jesus Christ."

Where did this incredible strength in the face of pain and loss come from? For Evelyn, it was partly from experiencing God's comfort in the past.

"Deep inside, I knew God was going to walk me through this somehow," she says. "I knew it because he'd walked with me through other crises earlier in my life."

One of those crises began shortly after Texas Tech University sweethearts Rick and Evelyn were married in 1982. They'd been trying to start a family without success. During the couple's first five years of marriage, Evelyn miscarried twice and began infertility treatments.

"After the second miscarriage, I went through depression," Evelyn says. "I prayed, 'God, take away my desire to be a mom if it isn't your will, because this is just so painful.' I had to let go and trust God with my future."

That experience helped Evelyn deal with the loss of her husband. "The past year I've had to take hold of God's hand and step out in faith into absolute blackness," she says. "I've gone way beyond the polite stages with God. I've yelled and cried out to Him with a deeper, gut-wrenching cry than ever before. But He's proven to me He's there, holding my hand as I take each step forward. That's why when you walk through a crisis, it's so important to have a foundation of faith already established. Because you have to know whose hand you're holding in order to step into the darkness of an uncertain future."

Not that it's always easy to take those steps. Last August, an independent investigation committee released its report on the cause of the *Columbia* explosion. The findings sent Evelyn reeling. While the committee concluded the shuttle ultimately broke apart because of a wing that was punctured during liftoff, it said NASA's careless, risk-taking culture was as much to blame for the accident as the damaged wing itself.

"If a meteor had hit them, or if something else catastrophic had happened, it would have been easier to deal with than an oversight," Evelyn says. "But there's a way NASA handles their management that needs to be changed. As a Christian, I have to figure out what to do with these realities. I'm on my face daily asking God to show me."

The report determined the astronauts probably lived for 30 seconds after the shuttle broke up and then died of blunt force and thermal injuries in association with exposure to extreme altitude.

"I thought I knew what would be in the report, but I didn't realize all the details it would include," Evelyn says. "I do better when I see things coming."

The moments when she's been overwhelmed with unexpected grief have been hardest to bear. "I remember one day shortly after the accident when we'd run out of milk," Evelyn says. "I walked in the grocery store and saw a magazine with a picture of Rick on the front and a headline that read, 'The last seven horrifying minutes for the space shuttle crew.' I saw Matthew looking at it. By the time we checked out, I was a hysterical, sobbing mess.

"Going to the grocery store is still one of the hardest things for me to do," Evelyn adds. "Rick used to buy this weird non-fat peanut butter that he loved to put in smoothies. And he loved to eat almonds. I go down the aisle now and think, I don't need to get those things. It's so painful."

The same pain that makes mundane tasks such as grocery shopping so draining has become the catalyst for Evelyn to reach others who suffer or who are struggling with their faith.

Women of Faith President Mary Graham says conference attendees love listening to Evelyn because she's honest about her imperfections and has a wonderful sense of humor. She's also the image of a survivor to women facing uncertain times.

"Evelyn didn't make it through this by turning out the lights and crawling under her bed, but by taking one tiny baby step of faith at a time," Mary says. "When women hear her stand up and say, 'I can make it through this crisis because what I believed about God in my head now has proven true in my heart,' then they think, *I can trust him with my everyday dramas, too.*"

Evelyn recounts her story of loss in *High Calling: The Courageous*

Life and Faith of Shuttle Columbia Commander Rick Husband (Thomas Nelson), which released in January. In it she describes Rick's faith and how God was at work in the moments leading up to the tragedy, providing precious memories for her and the kids to share with Rick before his mission.

Before he went into quarantine to prepare for the mission, Rick videotaped devotionals for the kids to watch every day during his trip. "Now they have on tape an hour-and-a-half of their dad talking to them about God," Evelyn says.

Rick also left Evelyn a journal he started for her in the weeks leading up to his mission. She keeps it by her nightstand.

"He wrote in it every single day until he left," she says. "It was very unlike him, but God was at work in his heart. Rick ended up giving me an account of the last days we had together."

On February 1, the one-year anniversary of the tragedy, Evelyn and her kids [traveled] to Washington, D.C., to dedicate a memorial to the *Columbia* astronauts in Arlington Cemetery. Standing next to the site is another memorial already established for the *Challenger* crew who perished in 1986.

"Three years ago, I went with Laura's fifth-grade class on a field trip to D.C., and Laura and I visited the *Challenger* memorial," Evelyn says. "I remember standing there with my arm around Laura begging God, *Never let it be us.*

"In light of what happened, you'd think I'd be disillusioned with God. But strangely, it hasn't been that way at all," she says. "I've learned Jesus was a man of sorrows who's well acquainted with my grief. He knows how deeply I'm mourning. And he's been with me every moment. He's also given me a real chance to honor him through this situation. That's what I'm trying to do."[20]

The Best Inspirational Quotes

If you're heading in the wrong direction,
God allows u-turns.

—Anonymous

You see things; and you say, "Why?" But I dream
things that never were; and I say, "Why not?"

—George Bernard Shaw

Dreaming about a thing in order to do it properly is
right; but dreaming about it when we should be
doing it is wrong.

—Oswald Chambers

A pessimist is one who makes difficulties of his
opportunities; an optimist is one who makes opportu-
nities of his difficulties.

—Reginald Mansell

The most untutored person with passion is more per-
suasive than the most eloquent without.

—Francois de La Rochefoucauld

You can make more friends in two months by becom-
ing interested in other people than you can in two
years by trying to get other people interested in you.

—Dale Carnegie

Class Act

BY MARY ANN O'ROARK

ORAL LEE BROWN IS no millionaire, just a hardworking mom. She grew up poor in Mississippi, where her family picked cotton before moving to California. She put herself through college while holding down a full-time job and raising three daughters. Once her girls were grown, she turned her energies to running a real-estate agency and a restaurant in Oakland.

One day in 1987 a little girl came up to Oral Lee on the street and asked for food. Oral Lee bought her a sandwich. "Why aren't you in school?" she asked, but the little girl ran off.

Oral Lee went to Brookfield, the closest elementary school, to ask about the girl. She ended up meeting a classroom of 23 first graders. Kids who, in the midst of the poverty- and crime-blighted neighborhood, seemed hungry most of all for inspiration. Suddenly an idea took hold. Oral Lee talked it over with her pastor and Brookfield's principal. Then she went back to that first-grade class.

"Who wants to be a dummy?" Oral Lee asked the children. "A drug dealer?" Silence. "Who wants to grow up and be somebody?" Every hand shot up. "If you stay in school and graduate, I'll send you to college. That's a promise."

Oral Lee made forty-five thousand dollars a year. She set aside a tithe for church and put away an additional ten thousand dollars a year in a trust fund for the Brookfield kids. Her most important investment? Oral Lee made herself part of the students' lives. She tutored them every week, organized field trips, got them books. She invited the kids to her house for birthdays and holidays (and for some of her famous peach cobbler) and shared her own climb out of poverty. She even flew some of them east on a tour of colleges when they started high school to remind them of the goal they were striving toward.

The kids didn't disappoint their beloved Mrs. Brown. Twenty of those 23 first graders graduated high school. Oral Lee's trust fund sent them to college. Even thousands of miles away from Oakland, they stayed in touch with their "Real Life Angel," as Jeffrey Toney titled a song he wrote in her honor while he was a student at Chicago's Columbia College. "I think God sent Mrs. Brown to me," Jeffrey says.

Last May Oral Lee watched the first of her class graduate from college. Latosha Hunter got her diploma from Alcorn State University in Mississippi, which she chose in part because it's near where her mentor grew up. "If she can make it, I can make it," Latosha says. Oral Lee has also supported the kids who took a different path. Cory Edwards, for one. He's training to become a firefighter.

Now Oral Lee has taken 60 more students under her wing— first, fifth and ninth graders chosen by Oakland school officials. She's set up a foundation and is assisted by volunteer mentors to make sure each student gets that crucial individual attention. Oral Lee will never forget these Brookfield first graders, though. "They still call and come see me," she says. "Those kids are my kids."[21]

The Best Inspirational Quotes

Live so that you wouldn't be ashamed to sell the family parrot to the town gossip.

—WILL ROGERS

The greatest mistake you can make in life is to be continually fearing you will make one.

—ELBERT G. HUBBARD

Render more service than that for which you are paid and you will soon be paid for more than you render. This is The Law of Increasing Returns.

—NAPOLEON HILL

The men who try to do something and fail are infinitely better than those who try nothing and succeed.

—LLOYD JONES

Train your child in the way in which you know you should have gone yourself.

—C. H. SPURGEON

As a mother, my job is to take care of the possible and trust God with the impossible.

—RUTH BELL GRAHAM

Attacked by Killer Bees

BY JOE PORTALE

OUR VW VAN BOUNCED violently over the rutted dirt road. As I peered through the dust-caked windshield my stomach growled. I glanced at my watch. We needed to find a spot for lunch, some shade in this desolate country.

I was leading a group of teens and young adults, including several nurses, on a mission to the outback of the West African country of Burkina Faso. Our small caravan was on its way to the bush village of Bouroum Bouroum. There were no other vehicles on the road—a fact that made me even more anxious to reach our destination.

I was tired of traveling. We had come thousands of miles, crossing the Sahara, following only the tall posts in the sand that marked the route. Now we bounced over a washboard trail on the parched African savanna. Dust was everywhere. When the windshield broke on one van, we had to wear thick bandannas around our mouths just to breathe.

Baobab trees studded the horizon—strange, dreary trees that looked as if they had sprouted upside down, with their gnarled and twisted branches stabbing the sky.

"Let's stop," I said, spotting a large baobab ahead. *About as much shade as we'll find.* Red dust billowed up as the vans jerked to a halt. Everyone got out and stretched, and a group set out our lunch. Lidia, a pretty dark-haired girl, spread old green army blankets on the ground.

While the rest of the group ate, I studied our surroundings. The air seemed oddly still. Cicadas buzzed. I thought I heard a dove coo in the brush. A grasshopper jumped across the blanket, scurrying for cover.

Along our route there had been times when I sensed God watching over us. Once, we had managed to find our way in a blinding sandstorm. At a desert oasis we had arrived just in time to help a Bedouin woman who almost died in childbirth. I felt especially close to God camping in the Sahara beneath the brilliant stars, but now He seemed far away. This place was too hot, too quiet, too empty. I had a strange feeling of unease.

"We've got to get going," I announced. We had many more miles to travel, and I was growing impatient. Everyone stood and gathered the blankets. Several of the girls filed behind the tree for a bathroom break.

Suddenly a piercing shriek came from behind the baobab. I sprinted over. Maybe some wild animal had attacked. Snakes? Scorpions? This land was full of them.

Then I heard it: A thick buzzing sound filled the air. All at once it came, a dark, menacing cloud. Bees. They attacked my ankles and swooped under my collar. They were finding every inch of my exposed skin. I closed my eyes and tried to brush them away. *Stay calm.* I slapped at my neck. A hot stinger pierced my cheek, and pain shot through my elbow. I flailed my arms frantically.

Bees! Killer bees!

I ran blindly. Anywhere to get away from the deadly, angry roar. I beat the air. The bees kept coming at me, stinging, buzzing. *Help! Get me out of here!*

I couldn't tell which way to turn. Trapped by the assault, I hardly dared open my eyes. All around me people were running and screaming.

I grabbed one girl by the arm and pulled her away from the baobab tree. The bees near her attacked my face. We dashed up the road, waving our arms, trying to outrun the cloud. My feet pounded the dirt as I ran away from the terrible noise.

Several guys carried a girl to us and laid her on the ground. It was Lidia. Everyone gathered around her. She was covered with writhing insects, their stingers pumping venom into her body. They were on her eyelids, in her ears, on her arms and hands. Bees buzzed in her long hair.

"I . . . can't . . . breathe," she gasped.

"Hang in there," one of the nurses said as she carefully removed dozens of stingers from the girl's body. Several others helped. Lidia's eyes rolled back and her head fell into the dust of the roadway.

I dropped to my knees. People were on the ground, retching, all around me. *What do I do?* Desperately, I wanted to pray. Desperately. But my thoughts were jumbled; no words came. I felt only fear and loneliness in this place. Forcing myself, I closed my eyes and spoke, "God, this isn't your fault. Your world is good and beautiful. . . ."

I couldn't believe my ears. The words were coming automatically. I was thanking God for His whole creation—His whole creation—even in the midst of this disaster. But something told me it was the right prayer. "Thank you, God, for these bees," I prayed.

"They are part of your world. You are gracious and good."

I opened my eyes. The wild buzzing had diminished. We picked stingers out of our skin. Bees still swarmed around our vans as though searching for their hive.

"We've got to get medicine," one of the nurses called. She knew there was some back in the van. She stood up from the dust. "I'll go," she said.

We watched as she staggered back, waving her arms. Darting into the van, she grabbed a medical kit. She ran back to Lidia and gave her a shot of antihistamine. "I don't think she's going to make it," someone said.

"Thank you, Lord, for your creation," I continued to pray. "For all of your creatures. Thank you for life."

One of our drivers covered himself with blankets and ran back to the vans. Opening the doors so the bees could fly out, he started one van and drove it to us. The van rocked from one side of the road to the other as he jerked the steering wheel to duck the angry bees.

"Thank you, God. . . ."

We chased the last of the bees out of the van and lowered Lidia's limp form on the back seat while drivers went for the other vehicles. I sat in front to keep an eye on her, and one of the nurses sat next to her, bathing her forehead with a cool, damp cloth. It would be several hours of rough driving before we reached the missionary infirmary.

An hour down the road, Lidia stirred. Jerking her arm toward her hair, she mumbled, "Cut . . . my . . . hair . . . off."

"It's okay, Lidia. We've pulled the bees out of your hair."

Her eyes opened. "Where am I?"

"You're in a van on your way to Bouroum Bouroum," I said.

She leaned weakly on one elbow. "I couldn't breathe. I felt my life leaving me. And I thought, *No, Lord, that's not fair to my parents.* When you began praying, a cool breeze swept over me and I was able to breathe again."

How had she heard me praying when she was unconscious? I wondered.

After two and a half hours on the road we arrived at the village, covered with red, swollen welts. We blurted out our story to the missionaries there.

"You are very fortunate," one of them told me as others tended to the most seriously injured people. "Not long ago another foreigner disturbed a hive of bees. He was stung more than 40 times and died."

That night I fell into my sleeping bag, exhausted. I kept playing the day over in my mind—how we had survived in this hot, dry, lonely land. Just then I felt thin grains of sand between my toes— the dust, as inescapable as God's mercy.

"Thank you, God," I prayed. "Thank you for the dust, the trees, the sand, the wind, the sun, the water, the bees. Your creation is full of mystery and goodness. But your mercy is mightiest of all."[22]

Alexandra Scott: She Has Big Dreams for Sick Kids

BY RONNIE POLANECZKY

SHE MAY NOT KNOW the expression "When life hands you lemons, make lemonade," but that's just what seven-year-old Alex Scott has done. For the past three years, she has raised funds for cancer research by selling lemonade from a stand in her front yard. She has also bravely lived the wisdom of the saying. Diagnosed as an infant with neuroblastoma—a cruelly aggressive form of childhood cancer—Alex has endured painful surgeries, radiation treatment, a stem cell transplant, and continual chemotherapy. But after each punishing treatment, she has rallied, because, as Alex explains, that's when she can "get back to being a kid."

The fund-raising started in the spring of 2000, when Alex, then four, told her parents—Liz Scott, 34, a stay-at-home mom, and Jay, 35, a medical textbook salesman—that she wanted to sell lemonade and donate the money to the Connecticut hospital where she was receiving treatment. Liz and Jay helped her make it happen, and Liz's sister arranged a little publicity in the local paper. On the day of the sale, however, they were amazed at how many people showed up, all wanting to meet Alex.

Since that first success, which earned $2,000, Alex has held three more sales. These days, her stand goes up in Wynnewood, Pennsylvania, where she and her parents moved, along with her brothers Patrick, nine, Eddie, five, and Joey, nine months, so Alex could be treated at Children's Hospital of Philadelphia.

As word of her mission spread partly via a Web site, alexslemonade.com, others were inspired to hold similar sales and forward the proceeds to the nonprofit fund, Alex's Lemonade Stand, which her family has set up to support cancer research. Its take to date? More than $150,000, with donations coming from an amazing range of supporters: an NBA honcho (Philadelphia 76ers General Manager Billy King), corporations (Volvo and Cigna), Brownie troops, and school classes. There was even a bride who, instead of buying flowers for her wedding, donated the money to Alex's fund—and used lemonade pitchers as centerpieces at her reception. "The response is like nothing we have ever experienced," says Phil Arkow, a spokesperson for the Philadelphia Foundation, which administers the fund.

It's easy to see why people who've met Alex dive right in to help. For all of her spunk, this shy, charming child is desperately sick. She has undergone every normal protocol for treatment of the many tumors she has developed—near her kidneys and liver; and on her spine and bones. Now, with her disease still advancing, doctors have to rely on newer therapies to keep Alex going. "As each drug runs its course, we're on the lookout for the next one that will work, until a permanent cure can be found," says Liz. "That's why it's so critically important to bring new treatments to the market."

The Scotts hope that their recent gift of $50,000 from Alex's fund to a neuroblastoma research team at Children's Hospital will help make that happen. The money will pay for a support staff, whose work should speed approval of promising drugs—ones that could buy more time for Alex and other kids with cancer.

Speaking for all of them, Alex explains, "We just want to play more." Because of her courage, she and thousands of other kids may get to do just that.[23]

Our Christmas Miracles

BY LISA COLLIER COOL

WHEN THE MORRIS FAMILY of Charlotte, North Carolina, trims their Christmas tree this year, one ornament in particular will get a prominent place on a high branch.

It's not the prettiest ornament in their collection or even the oldest. Truth be told, it's kind of tacky: a ceramic tropical fish with oversized lips and "Tampa" printed along the bottom. But the souvenir will always have special meaning because that's where the family spent Christmas two years ago, as Amy Morris underwent a rare surgery to save the lives of her unborn twins.

The 2001 holiday season started out joyous and hopeful, with Amy and her friends throwing their annual "Happy Birthday, Jesus" party in early December. And everyone was excited about Amy's routine four-month prenatal exam later that week, when she and her husband, Tom, would learn the sex of their twins.

"When the ultrasound showed they were boys, Tom and I were thrilled because we already had a girl," says the 32-year-old former real estate paralegal and now stay-at-home mom. A minute later the doctor discovered a terrible problem. "He said the pregnancy was in danger. The chance of losing both babies was a hundred percent if nothing was done. We were both in shock."

The babies had twin-to-twin transfusion syndrome (TTTS), a rare pregnancy complication that only strikes identical twins, Amy's doctor explained. Fetuses with this condition have a shared placenta with faulty blood vessels that allow one twin to receive too much blood, triggering a wide range of disorders for both the babies and the mother. For the larger twin, called the recipient, the increased blood supply sends the heart and kidneys into overdrive trying to rid the body of the excess fluid. This causes the amniotic sac to swell like a water balloon, sometimes growing so dangerously large that the fetus, and sometimes the mother, goes into congestive heart failure.

The "donor" twin, on the other hand, has so little fluid to move in that it may appear stuck to the uterine wall, as if encased in shrink-wrap. Usually very small, these fetuses often show no visible bladder during ultrasound exams, as was the case with Amy's unborn son. As the disorder progresses, the baby gives away so much of its blood supply that it can develop severe anemia, followed by heart failure. About 6,000 American babies a year are affected by TTTS, and 4,000 of them die.

While there are some treatments for the condition, Amy's doctor advised against them. Because she was only 16 weeks along on that December day, it was too early for serial amniocentesis, a procedure in which excess fluid is drained from the bloated sac of the recipient twin.

Another possibility was fetal surgery. However, this procedure is performed for TTTS at only five hospitals in the United States. "I asked the doctor how many patients he'd sent for this operation," says Amy. "He said none, because it's so experimental. Then I asked if there was anything we could do, and he said no. If this had happened later in the pregnancy, he could have delivered the twins and maybe saved one. I was devastated and just fell apart."

Although the perinatologist proposed a wait-and-see approach, with weekly monitoring of the fetuses' condition, Amy and Tom, a 35-year-old engineer, were desperate to find something that could save their twins. "I said, 'What's going to happen if we wait? Things are only going to get worse,'" says Amy. The expectant parents consulted two specialists in high-risk pregnancy, who both agreed with the first doctor: Fetal surgery was just too new and risky to consider.

Amy and Tom went online and found the Web site of the Twin-to-Twin Transfusion Syndrome Foundation, a support and resource group for parents whose kids are affected by TTTS (www.tttsfoundation.org). They contacted the foundation, which immediately sent the Morrises detailed information about the new surgery, along with the names and phone numbers of several women who had actually had it. After talking to some of these patients and hearing their success stories, the expectant parents became convinced that fetal surgery wasn't as dangerous as Amy's doctor had made it out to be. And, adds Tom, "It was our babies' only hope."

But there was yet another problem. The Morrises learned of a doctor in Florida who had invented an in utero operation for TTTS, but his procedure was ideally performed after the 18th week of pregnancy. That meant Amy would have to wait another two weeks, if her babies could make it that long. "It was very hard to feel them moving inside me and know I could lose them both tomorrow," she says.

During the anxious wait, the expectant parents went back to Amy's original doctor. Although he was still skeptical about fetal surgery, he agreed to send her records to Rubén Quintero, M.D., medical director of the Florida Institute for Fetal Diagnosis and Therapy at St. Joseph's Women's Hospital in Tampa. Dr. Quintero's procedure involves inserting a narrow laser through a tiny incision in the woman's abdomen and uterus to seal off the vessels that cause abnormal blood flow between the twins. So far, he's done about 250 TTTS operations, with an 84 percent survival rate for one baby and 50 percent for both. About 2 percent of the survivors develop neurological complications.

The following week, the situation took a turn for the worse. "The second baby's membrane was wrapped around him like a shroud," Amy says. "The only place where the doctor could find any fluid at all was between his fingers. And the baby was so crammed against the wall of my uterus that he couldn't move his arms or even kick his legs." The test results were sent to Dr. Quintero, whose nurse immediately called Amy's perinatologist and told him that the Morrises needed to come to Florida Institute on December 25, when Amy would finally hit the 18-week mark. "I said, 'But that's Christmas! Are things really that bad?' She said there was a very narrow window to save the twins."

What would the couple tell their 2-year-old daughter, Lacy, who was gleefully anticipating Santa's arrival? They decided to have an early celebration on Christmas Eve. Then Amy spent hours on the phone, trying unsuccessfully to find out if her insurance would cover the $25,000 operation. She and Tom decided that if they had to, they'd charge it on their credit cards and worry about the bills later. That evening, the couple made a special trip to their church to pray for the operation's success.

Early Christmas morning, the Morrises and several of their relatives flew to Tampa. Before checking into the hospital, Amy kissed

Lacy, who had accompanied them, goodbye. "I was crying because I knew there was some risk to me, and I didn't know if I'd see her again." And if Dr. Quintero couldn't save both babies, he'd have to tie off the umbilical cord of the weaker twin to stop the abnormal flow, which would result in that baby's death.

By this point, tests showed that the donor twin was in desperate danger, with only intermittent blood flow to his heart. Surgery was scheduled for the following morning. Before the operation, Tom held Amy's hand and told her over and over that he loved her. "We'll get through this together," he promised as she was wheeled away to the operating room. Half an hour later, Dr. Quintero was back with good news. The procedure had gone smoothly and Amy was fine. While the expectant mother was in the OR, the Morrises' insurance company called and agreed to cover the entire cost.

On December 27, Amy lay on an exam table as an ultrasound wand was moved across her belly. Tom and Dr. Quintero were by her side, as the technician announced, "We have a heartbeat for Baby A," then added several seconds later, "We have a heartbeat for Baby B, too!" The Morrises were elated, but the doctor warned that things could still go wrong. Amy was now well enough to go home to North Carolina, but as a precaution she was put on bed rest for a month.

Back in Charlotte, the couple was relieved when an ultrasound test showed that Baby B, the donor twin, finally had a visible bladder. Another test a month later brought even better results: Both boys were thriving, and Baby B now had plenty of fluid to swim in. Although Amy's OB/GYN was concerned that she might deliver prematurely, as frequently happens after fetal surgery, she amazed him by making it to 37 weeks, when the boys were large enough to be delivered by C-section.

On May 14, 2002, Amy gave birth to Joseph Edwin Morris, who weighed in at 8 pounds, 5 ounces, and John Thomas Morris, who was 6 pounds, 2 ounces. "We were ecstatic!" exclaims the proud mom. "Everyone was amazed when they put the babies on the scale. The entire room gasped because Joseph was so large for a twin." Both boys were also in excellent health. . . . Amy says their mental and physical development has been completely normal. "They're so happy that they smile all the time," she says, "And Lacy is great with them."

One boy is still taking from the other, but now it's the other way around. "John is a pistol," says Amy with a laugh. "As soon as Joe puts the pacifier in his mouth, John takes it away while poor Joe just sits and cries. The tables have definitely turned!"[24]

The Best Inspirational Quotes

What sunshine is to flowers, smiles are to humanity.
They are but trifles, to be sure, but scattered along
life's pathway, the good they do is inconceivable.
—JOSEPH ADDISON

"I can forgive, but I cannot forget," is only another
way of saying, "I will not forgive." Forgiveness ought
to be like a canceled note – torn in two, and burned
up, so that it never can be shown against one.
—HENRY WARD BEECHER

Worry is like a rocking chair: It gives you something
to do, but doesn't get you anywhere.
—ANONYMOUS

I remember my mother's prayers and they have
always followed me.
They have clung to me all my life.
—ABRAHAM LINCOLN

Look around you and be distressed, look within you
and be depressed, look to Jesus and be at rest.
—ANONYMOUS

Kind words can be short and easy to speak, but their
echoes are truly endless.
—MOTHER TERESA

Is My Sister Going to Die?

BY CAMILLA BEKIUS

I HEARD THE QUIVER in Mom's voice as she took a deep breath and pressed her hands together to stop them from shaking. My stomach twisted into a tight knot as she told our family what we'd suspected for a long time: "The tests came back positive. Allysa has the HIV virus." I couldn't move as I sat there, waiting for it to sink in. As a missionary family living in Brazil, we had decided to adopt a baby from a local orphanage. Because of the mother's background, we knew there was a possibility that the baby might have been born with a sexually transmitted disease. But we hadn't been sure—until now. As I listened to my parents talk about the seriousness of Allysa's illness, I could only think about one thing: HIV turns into AIDS, and people die when they get AIDS. Allysa is going to die.

It was the day before Thanksgiving, a time to give thanks for the good things in my life. But what did I have to be thankful for? I wanted to cry, to scream at the world. But I didn't. I just sat there cross-legged on the floor of our living room, too stunned to know what to do.

In the silence, my siblings and I looked at our 8-month old sister, grinning and giggling on my dad's lap. She had no idea why she was suddenly the center of attention. In the awful silence she continued to laugh and wave her arms up and down at us, enjoying every minute she had in the spotlight.

As we all sat around the living room staring at Allysa, not knowing what to say or do, Mom choked back tears and tried to control her voice as she explained how the HIV virus would eventually become AIDS. She told us that people don't actually die of AIDS but that it lowers the immune system's ability to keep away diseases. People with AIDS usually die of pneumonia or some other contracted sickness that their body can't fight off. So Allysa could survive for years, Mom said, living a pretty normal life before the HIV became AIDS. Or she could die in a year or two.

I watched my brother bite his lip and my sister Erica and my mom wipe away tears. I wanted to cry, to feel the relief of tears running down my face, but tears wouldn't come. My dad began to pray, his voice faltering as he tried to force the words past the tears and tightness in his throat. Finally, when he could no longer speak, my mom continued for him.

"Lord, we don't understand why these things are happening, but we ask that you be with us and help us through this. And Lord, we thank you for Allysa, the life you've given us and the joy she's brought our family."

The next day I walked into our mission center's annual Thanksgiving potluck. Dazed and bewildered, I watched friends come by our table and talk to my parents, crying and praying with them, holding Allysa. It seemed like everyone we knew showed up, and my parents would talk to each person, only taking a bite of food when someone else was talking.

As I watched Allysa being cuddled and held by our friends, I thought about the day we brought her home from the orphanage. She was only two months old, malnourished and sick with malaria. She had looked like a little old man, shriveled and curled up in a baby seat that almost swallowed her whole. Her Brazilian features—tan skin, black hair, dark eyes—were quite a contrast with the rest of her new blond-haired, blue-eyed family. She had a smile that would have melted an ice cube.

My parents had prayed intensely for a year before they decided to adopt a child from the nearby orphanage. We were sure God had given this baby girl to our family, yet now it seemed she was going to die. My thoughts were a tangle of confused questions and hurt.

What could Allysa have ever done to deserve this?

Why was she forced to pay for the mistakes of a mother who'd simply dumped her out at an orphanage without once looking back?

The worst thing about it was that there was nothing I could do to make her better.

During the weeks that followed the test results, I watched as my parents loved and cared for my little sister. They bought rubber gloves to deal with any bleeding and did their best to keep her away from all possible sickness. In all of their pain and hurt, they seemed to put their trust fully in God. I could see it in their prayers, in their tears, and in their efforts to protect her from illness. They didn't understand why this was happening any more than I did, but they trusted that God would bring our family through this.

One day I watched as Dad played on the floor with Allysa. Dad growled at her in mock anger as she tugged at his beard. She laughed. She pulled. He growled louder. She laughed louder and pulled harder.

Without a second thought, I soon found myself on the floor with Dad and my baby sister. I joined in the fun, tickling her feet and round tummy, listening to her laughter fill the house.

Suddenly, I felt relief. The burden of all the questions and emotions I'd been carrying around was lifted from me. It was like peace had returned to my heart. Feelings I hadn't experienced for a long time rushed through me. I felt a genuine joy, even through the pain. God was still there. I knew it. Like my parents had done all along, I could trust him. Even as I hurt and failed to understand why my sister was sick, I could trust him. I wasn't alone in my pain. He was there for me, providing a glimpse of his love through the giggles of a tiny baby.

Even though my parents were willing to accept Allysa's illness, they also had some doubts about how accurate her diagnosis had been. So three weeks later, they decided to move us back to the United States where we could take advantage of better, more advanced medical tests. There was a chance, a slim chance, that our doctors in Brazil had missed something. Soon Allysa was visiting doctors once again, having her blood drawn and analyzed. It took two long weeks to hear the results.

I was sitting at our kitchen table making cookies when the call from the doctor came. Mom and I were the only ones home. When she picked up the phone, I leaned over her shoulder, straining to hear every word. I couldn't pick up much of what was being said. But I watched as relief spread over my mother's face. Then she turned around and looked at me, and slowly repeated the doctor's words back to him.

"The tests came back negative."

It finally registered. My baby sister did not have the HIV virus!

After hugging and crying—and accidentally burning the chocolate chip cookies—Mom and I frantically rushed around the kitchen, shoving cookie dough in the fridge, finding hats, coats and keys before rushing out to our old blue van. We must have broken every speed limit on the road as we drove to Dad's part-time job to tell him the news.

My sister would live to have beard-pulling contests and tickling matches for years to come. My sister would live. That's all I could think about. My sister would live.

Thank you, God.

Camilla wrote this story during an internship with Campus Life. She and her family recently returned to their missionary work in Brazil.[25]

The Dying Drummer Boy

BY DR. M.L. ROSVALLY

I WAS A SURGEON in the United States Army during the Civil War. After the battle of Gettysburg, there were hundreds of wounded soldiers in my hospital. Many were wounded so severely that a leg or an arm, or sometimes both, needed to be amputated.

One of these was a boy who had only been in the service for three months. Since he was too young to be a soldier, he had enlisted as a drummer. When my assistants came to give him chloroform before the amputation, he turned his head and refused it. When they told him that it was the doctor's orders, he said, "Send the doctor to me."

I came to his bedside and said, "Young man, why do you refuse the chloroform? When I found you on the battlefield, you were so far gone that I almost didn't bother to pick you up. But when you opened those large blue eyes, it occurred to me that you had a mother somewhere who might be thinking of you at that very moment. I didn't want you to die on the field, so I had you brought here. But you've lost so much blood that you're just too weak to live through an operation without chloroform. You'd better let me give you some."

He laid his hand on mine, looked me in the face and said, "Doctor, one Sunday afternoon, when I was nine and a half years old, I received Jesus Christ as my Saviour. I learned to trust Him then, and I've been trusting Him ever since. I know I can trust Him now. He is my strength. He will support me while you amputate my arm and leg."

I asked him if he would at least let me give him a little brandy. Again, he looked at me and said, "Doctor, when I was about five years old, my mother knelt by my side, with her arms around me, and said, 'Charlie, I am praying to Jesus that you will never take even one drink of alcohol. Your father died a drunkard, and I've asked God to use you to warn people against the dangers of drinking and to encourage them to love and serve the Lord.' I am now 17 years old, and I have never had anything stronger than tea or coffee. There is a very good chance that I am about to die and go into the presence of my God. Would you send me there with brandy on my breath?"

I will never forget the look that boy gave me. At that time I hated Jesus, but I respected the boy's loyalty to his Saviour. And when I saw how he loved and trusted Him to the very end, something deeply touched my heart. I did for that boy what I had never done for any other solder—I asked him if he wanted to see his chaplain.

Chaplain R. knew the boy well from having seen him frequently at the tent prayer meetings. Taking his hand, he said, "Charlie, I'm really sorry to see you like this."

"Oh, I'm all right, sir," Charlie answered. "The doctor offered me chloroform, but I told him I didn't want any. Then he wanted to give me some brandy, which I didn't want either. So now, if my

Saviour calls me, I can go to Him in my right mind."

"You might not die, Charlie," said the chaplain, "but if the Lord does call you home, is there anything I can do for you after you're gone?"

"Chaplain, please reach under my pillow and take my little Bible. My mother's address is inside. Please send it to her, and write a letter for me. Tell her that since I left home, I have never let a single day pass—no matter if we were on the march, on the battlefield, or in the hospital—without reading a portion of God's Word, and daily praying that He would bless her."

"Is there anything else I can do for you, my lad?" asked the chaplain. "Yes—please write a letter to the Sunday school teacher of the Sands Street Church in Brooklyn, New York. Tell him that I've never forgotten his encouragement, good advice, and many prayers for me. They have helped and comforted me through all the dangers of battle. And now, in my dying hour, I thank the Lord for my dear old teacher, and ask Him to bless and strengthen him. That is all."

Then turning to me, he said, "I'm ready, doctor. I promise I won't even groan while you take off my arm and leg, if you don't offer me chloroform." I promised, but I didn't have the courage to take the knife in my hand without first going into the next room and taking a little brandy myself.

While cutting through the flesh, Charlie Coulson never groaned. But when I took the saw to separate the bone, the lad took the corner of his pillow in his mouth, and all I could hear him whisper was, "O Jesus, blessed Jesus! Stand by me now." He kept his promise. He never groaned.

I couldn't sleep that night. Whichever way I tossed and turned, I saw those soft blue eyes, and when I closed my own eyes, the words, "Blessed Jesus, stand by me now," kept ringing in my ears. A little after midnight, I finally left my bed and visited the hospital— a thing I had never done before unless there was an emergency. I had such a strange and strong desire to see that boy. When I got there, an orderly told me that 16 of the badly wounded soldiers had died. "Was Charlie Coulson one of them?" I asked. "No, sir," he answered, "he's sleeping as sweetly as a babe."

When I came to his bed, one of the nurses said that at about nine o'clock, two members of the Y.M.C.A. came through the hospital to read and sing a hymn. Chaplain R. was with them, and he knelt by Charlie's bed and offered up a fervent and soul-stirring prayer. Then, while still on their knees, they sang one of the sweetest of all hymns, "Jesus, Lover Of My Soul." Charlie sang along with them, too. I couldn't understand how that boy, who was in such horrible pain, could sing.

Five days after I performed the operation, Charlie sent for me, and it was from him that I heard my first Gospel sermon. "Doctor," he said, "my time has come. I don't expect to see another sunrise. I want to thank you with all my heart for your kindness to me. I know you are Jewish and that you don't believe in Jesus, but I want you to stay with me and see me die trusting my Saviour to the last moment of my life." I tried to stay, but I just couldn't. I didn't have the courage to stand by and see a Christian boy die rejoicing in the love of that Jesus who I hated. So I hurriedly left the room.

About 20 minutes later an orderly came and found me sitting in my office with my hands covering my face. He told me that Charlie wanted to see me. "I've just seen him," I answered, "and I can't see him again."

"But, Doctor, he says he must see you once more before he dies."

So I made up my mind to go and see Charlie, say an endearing word, and let him die. However, I was determined that nothing he could say would influence me in the least bit, so far as his Jesus was concerned.

When I entered the hospital I saw he was sinking fast, so I sat down by his bed. Asking me to take his hand, he said, "Doctor, I love you because you are a Jew. The best friend I have found in this world was a Jew." I asked him who that was, and he answered, "Jesus Christ, and I want to introduce you to Him before I die. Will you promise me, doctor, that what I am about to say to you, you will never forget?" I promised, and he said, "Five days ago, while you amputated my arm and leg, I prayed to the Lord Jesus Christ and asked Him to make His love known to you."

Those words went deep into my heart. I couldn't understand how, when I was causing him the most intense pain, he could forget all about himself and think of nothing but his Saviour and my unconverted soul. All I could say to him was, "Well, my dear boy, you will soon be all right." With these words I left him, and 12 minutes later he fell asleep, "safe in the arms of Jesus."

Hundreds of soldiers died in my hospital during the war, but I only followed one to the grave, and that was Charlie Coulson. I rode three miles to see him buried. I had him dressed in a new uniform, and placed in an officer's coffin, with a United States flag over it.

That boy's dying words made a deep impression upon me. I was rich at that time so far as money was concerned, but I would have given every penny I possessed if I could have felt toward Christ as Charlie did. But that feeling cannot be bought with money. Alas, I soon forgot all about my Christian soldier's little sermon, but I could not forget the boy himself. Looking back, I now know that I was under deep conviction of sin at that time. But for nearly 10 years, I fought against Christ with all the hatred I had, until finally the dear boy's prayer was answered, and I surrendered my life to the love of Jesus.

About a year and a half after my conversion, I went to a prayer meeting one evening in Brooklyn. It was at one of those meetings where Christians testify about the faithfulness of God. After several had spoken, an elderly lady stood up and said, "Dear friends, this may be the last time I have a chance to publicly share how good the Lord has been to me. My doctor told me yesterday that my right lung is nearly gone, and my left lung is failing fast, so at the best I only have a short time to be with you. But what is left of me belongs to Jesus. It's a great joy to know that I shall soon meet my son with Jesus in heaven.

"Charlie was not only a soldier for his country, but also a soldier for Christ. He was wounded at the battle of Gettysburg, and was cared for by a Jewish doctor, who amputated his arm and leg. He died five days after the operation. The chaplain of the regiment wrote me a letter, and sent me my boy's Bible. I was told that in his dying hour, my Charlie sent for that Jewish doctor, and said to him, 'Doctor, before I die I wish to tell you that five days ago, while you amputated my arm and leg, I prayed to the Lord Jesus Christ for you.'"

As I heard this lady speak, I just couldn't sit still! I left my seat, ran across the room, and taking her hand said, "God bless you, my dear sister. Your boy's prayer has been heard and answered! I am the Jewish doctor that Charlie prayed for, and his Saviour is now my Saviour! The love of Jesus has won my soul!"[26]

Esther Ahn Kim

BY CHRISTIN DITCHFIELD

$\mathcal{T}$ORTURE, IMPRISONMENT, death. When we think of
these atrocities committed against Christians during World War
II, we immediately picture Nazi concentration camps. Countless
Christians lost their lives for sheltering Jews and refusing to support Hitler's evil regime. Although they were not aware of it,
thousands of their brothers and sisters in Christ were also losing
their lives for the sake of the Gospel—in Korea.

Japan had occupied Korea for more than 30 years. As the
Japanese sought favor from their Shinto gods and goddesses during
World War II, they began to crack down on Korean Christians.
Japanese officials required every Korean home to display a Japanese
god in a place of honor. Miniature shrines were installed in every
school, business, and church. Those who refused to bow before the
idols risked cruel abuse at the hands of the government. Missionaries, pastors, and church leaders were particularly singled out for
unspeakable torture.

Ahn Ei Sook was a young woman teaching music at a Christian
mission school in Korea. She watched events unfold with a growing sense of horror. Miss Ahn had been raised in a household

divided by conflicting faiths. Her father was a wealthy business-man. He recognized the inherent danger of living in an occupied country and insisted his young daughter learn to speak the Japanese language fluently. He sent her to school in Japan, to ensure that she would be well-educated and well-received in any society. But Ahn's father had little interest in spiritual matters. He followed the traditions of his ancestors and carried out the rituals of idol worship—though he drew no hope or comfort or guidance from his faith.

Ahn's mother, on the other hand, was a devout Christian woman. She made sure her daughter had a saving knowledge of Jesus Christ, from the start. Ahn faithfully attended church with her mother, fellowshipping with other believers. She learned more than 150 hymns and studied countless Bible passages. Ahn's mother deeply impressed upon her the importance of staying true to her faith.

Now Miss Ahn was about to face her first real test. Once a month, all the local schools were ordered to make a pilgrimage up the mountain to the shrine of a Japanese goddess. On previous occasions, Ahn had feigned illness or come up with another excuse to avoid what she called "the indignity and blasphemy of bowing before the shrine." This time, the school principal came looking for her.

"Think about it, Miss Ahn," the principal said. "Is there any believer in Christ who wants to bow to heathen gods? We all hate to do such a thing, but we Christians are being persecuted with a power too ruthless to stand against. Unless we worship at the Japanese shrine, they will close this school!"

Ahn thought about the consequences of publicly refusing to bow to the goddess. She also thought of Shadrach and Meschach and

Abednego and what they had told King Nebuchadnezzar, as recorded in the third chapter of Daniel.

"Even if God did not save them from the burning fire . . . they would die honoring Him," Ahn recalled. "I was going to make the same decision. With God's help, I would never bow before the Japanese idol, even if He did not save me from the hands of the Japanese. I was saved by Jesus. I could bow only before God, the Father of my Saviour."

All the way to the shrine, she prayed for strength and courage: "Today on the mountain, before the large crowd . . . I will proclaim that there is no other God beside You. This is what I will do for Your holy name."

When the official gave the signal, everyone in the crowd bowed low before the shrine. Everyone, that is, except Ahn. In one sense, it was exhilarating. Ahn could feel the presence of God as she stood tall, her eyes firmly fixed on the heavens. But she knew that her defiance could not go unnoticed.

"As we made our way back to the school my heart was overshadowed by a dark cloud. Everyone had seen me refuse to bow to the shrine. I would be dragged to the police station and kicked and beaten until my eyes would come out. Even as a child I had never been so much as scolded. I wondered if I could stand being whipped and hearing those swaggering men blaspheme the name of Jesus. I could honestly say that I was not afraid of dying, but I feared being tortured without dying. How long could this body endure? What if I gave up my faith under the relentless torture? Just thinking of it made me so faint I could hardly see where I was walking. But I could not retreat. I had to fight."

Sure enough, the police were waiting for her at the school. But at the police station, Ahn was left alone in an official's office.

Amazingly, she managed to slip out of the crowded building and escape. For the next few months, Ahn and her mother lived like fugitives. They hid in little cottages in remote villages. Knowing that the police would catch up with her eventually, Ahn began to prepare herself to withstand imprisonment and torture. She practiced sleeping without blankets in the cold; she forced herself to eat rotten scraps of food, and even fast for days at a time. Ahn spent hours committing chapters and entire books of the Bible to memory—knowing that one day, her Bible would be taken from her.

As she continued to witness the brutal oppression of believers all around her, Ahn sensed God calling her to undertake a special mission. Someone needed to speak up about the atrocities. The Japanese government needed to be warned that God would judge them if they did not repent of their persecution of Korean Christians. Reading the Scriptures, Ahn became convinced that God's judgment would indeed fall upon them, like "sulfur fire from the sky." A Methodist leader named Elder Park shared Ahn's burden to warn the Japanese—but he did not speak the language.

As local believers gathered together to seek God's will, they became convinced that, like Esther in the Bible, Ahn had been called "for such a time as this." She could speak for Elder Park and herself and the people of Korea. Ahn knew that her life was already forfeited to Christ. She agreed to go to Tokyo with Elder Park, saying as Esther did: "If I perish, I perish."

Amazingly, Ahn and Park managed to penetrate the security of the Japanese Diet and deliver their startling announcement before the entire Japanese government. Many Japanese Christians were appalled—they had no idea what had been going on in Korea. But nothing could save Ahn from prison this time.

Returned to Korea, Ahn spent the next six years in the most terrible, inhumane conditions of the Japanese prisons. She battled sickness and starvation; she witnessed the horrific abuse of other prisoners. Time and time again, Ahn was called to testify before jailors, supervisors, and officials. She helped many of them make professions of faith in Christ. Others were dumbfounded by her faith and courage. They returned her to her cell unharmed. One official asked Ahn to write down her thoughts and observations on her imprisonment. She powerfully articulated the innocence of Christian prisoners and the injustices done to them. She described the brutality they suffered in gripping detail. To her astonishment, Ahn learned that her report was copied and distributed to officials at Japanese prisons all over Korea. New policies were instituted that lessened the torture of believers and resulted in some of the cruelest jailers being fired.

In her filthy cell, Ahn ministered to the other prisoners, comforting and discipling them. Every day, she prepared herself for death. There were moments when she felt incredible peace and joy at the prospect of giving her life for Jesus. In other moments, she battled discouragement and fear. Every time she was called before a judge, she knew her testimony could lead to her execution. But her life was repeatedly spared. She continued to boldly speak the truth, and God's favor rested heavily upon her. Soon Christians all over Korea and Japan had heard of Miss Ahn. So had the jailers, policemen, and government officials.

Ahn fully expected to become a martyr and die for her faith, but God had other plans. When World War II ended, the Japanese abandoned Korea. Ahn and the other prisoners were set free. Ahn learned that fire had indeed rained down from the sky—upon Hiroshima and Nagasaki. She would see with her own eyes the devastation and destruction. Ahn immediately began writing down everything that she had experienced. Her account became a best-selling book in Korea, China, and Japan. Eventually, Ahn married a Christian pastor—Don Kim. Together they traveled all over the United States and Europe, speaking at churches and sharing Ahn's testimony. "Esther" Ahn Kim wanted the world to know, in her words, "how Jesus loved those who loved Him; how He gave them strength to overcome the power of darkness; and how, in His unfailing mercy, He helped believers to have faith in Him."

She said, "I, too, knew His love and strength and peace. I would share it all with you . . . I cannot explain how such a weak woman as I was given such wonderful blessings during times of fear and suffering . . . the record of my prison life [is] a testimony of the acts of Jesus Christ."

Ahn Kim dedicated her life to sharing this message. As she had so often prayed, "Jesus, let me offer this humble testimony to You. I love You with my all."[27]

The Tender Mercy of Cheryl Kane

BY ELIZABETH GEHRMAN

SHE WAS A NUN. Then she was a wife. Now she devotes herself to helping the truly despairing. One woman's journey from a convent to the mean streets of Boston.

It was mid-October in Boston, one of those New England days so cold and windy, your eyes start to water the moment you step outdoors. Cheryl Kane was in search of Jack, an often-homeless alcoholic who had disappeared from the hospital.

Earlier that day, she'd learned that the 70-year-old man—hospitalized after suffering a massive coronary—had checked himself out too early, against the advice of the medical staff, while wearing only a sweatshirt vest and a hospital gown.

Cheryl had a good idea where Jack was. And so she snapped on her fanny pack—filled with dressings for wounds, a thermometer, antibiotic creams, and a blood pressure cuff—and grabbed some clothes and an extra winter coat from her closet.

Cheryl Kane, 52, is a member of the street outreach team of the Boston Health Care for the Homeless Program. On that day, she headed for Atlantic Avenue in downtown Boston. Near a construction site, she found Jack huddled between two concrete barriers.

But when Cheryl handed the shivering man the coat, a bright yellow parka, he recoiled.

"Where'd you get that?" wailed Jack. ". . . everyone will be able to see me in that."

"It's my husband's coat," Cheryl told him. "If you wear it, it'll keep you warm."

Uncertain, the homeless man asked, "Doesn't he want it anymore?"

"No, Jack, my husband died," Cheryl replied.

That sentence transformed Jack's whole demeanor. Grasping Cheryl's hands, he said, "Oh, honey, I'm so sorry. Go to that Dunkin' Donuts down the street and buy yourself a coffee—on me. Then come back and tell me about your husband."

Cheryl did as he suggested—paying for the coffee herself, of course—and then sat down on a milk crate next to Jack, who was now wearing the yellow parka. First she told him about another medical program he should enter. Then she talked a little about her husband, Jim, the man she'd loved dancing with, cheek to cheek, in their living room. Her anniversary date was approaching, and Cheryl was not looking forward to it. But the conversation with Jack helped.

Her marriage was part of an earlier life, before she started spending her days on the streets, supplying homeless men and women with desperately needed medical care.

And then there was the time before her marriage, when she had devoted herself to God. For Cheryl Kane's life has been a very long journey. . . .

"I went into the religious life at 19," says Cheryl, who has short blond hair and luminous blue eyes. "As a kid I had always been drawn to people in the world who needed help. I went to Catholic schools in Boston, and I saw the difference the sisters made in people's lives." She decided to enter the 130-year-old order of the Missionary Franciscan Sisters of the Immaculate Conception.

Her parents were upset at first. Cheryl was the oldest child and only daughter of John and Elinore Donahue. "My parents had the feeling I would enter the convent and they would never see me again," she says. And indeed, Cheryl was allowed visits from her parents only once a month at first; telephone calls were permitted every two weeks.

But while Cheryl was still in her early 20s, her religious order, like many others, relaxed its rules. Restrictions on family visits were dropped. "My parents could see how happy I was and how I loved the ideals that we stood for, of simplicity in life and spirituality," she recalls.

Over the next 20 years, Cheryl straddled two worlds, living in the convent but working in the community. She taught in Catholic schools, counseled young people, and did pastoral outreach, which meant talking about God not only in people's homes, but in hospitals and jails. She always felt at ease with the most downtrodden people and was never frightened by them, even when they were angry or delusional.

When she hit her early 40s, however, Cheryl started to feel restless, and she wondered more and more if she would be happier outside the convent. Obviously, leaving a religious life is a huge decision, and she spent a lot of time agonizing over it. One coworker friend she turned to was Jim Kane, a Jesuit priest. He told Cheryl to follow her heart. "I was afraid I was breaking my commitment to God; Jim helped me see that I was really being faithful to His plan for my life," she says now. Her decision was made.

Cheryl's first priority after leaving was to begin working with the homeless. She took a position at St. Francis House, a shelter in downtown Boston, doing job counseling for young adults. After deciding that the most effective way she could help was as a nurse, she started applying to various programs.

What Cheryl didn't know was that Jim was also striking out on a new path. "He had never let me know, in the whole time I was exploring my own questions about leaving, that it was something he had been contemplating off and on for ten years," she says.

During a leave of absence that he took to care for his ailing mother, Jim told Cheryl about his soul-searching. "I liked being with him," she says. "But I didn't want to spend too much time in case he went back to his order. I wanted him to make his decision freely—and I knew where my heart was going." Although she couldn't admit it to anyone, not even to herself, Cheryl had fallen in love. And when first love hits after 40, it hits hard.

Three years after Jim left the priesthood, he and Cheryl were married. She was midway through her nursing studies; Jim worked in the admissions office at Boston College. They were incredibly happy. "Jim and Cheryl understood that this was something extraordinary that they never pictured happening to them," says Leo Sullivan, a former colleague of Jim's. But, adds Sullivan, "There's something about fate, that some things are almost too good to be true. And this falls into that category."

One day Jim called Cheryl from work, saying he was getting a "wicked headache." He asked her to name for him the women he worked with; she did, and he repeated the names back to her. Then he asked the same question again.

"I asked Jim, 'Do you know who I am?'" Cheryl recalls, "and he said, 'I know you're my wife, but I can't think of your name.'"

Cheryl called his boss, and by the time she had hung up the phone and tried to call her husband back, Jim had had two seizures. Fifteen months after their wedding, he was diagnosed with a type of brain tumor that is fast growing and nearly always fatal.

As Jim's illness progressed, Cheryl's fear was compounded by her exhaustion—she was coping with not only the physical strain of taking care of him but also the emotional challenge of remaining outwardly upbeat while knowing how serious the illness was. And she was angry with God. *How could He place this wonderful man in my life and heart,* she asked herself, *and then rip him away from me?* For a time she tried to shut God out, but her faith was too strong, and she realized she needed Him more than ever.

Jim underwent brain surgery in January 1997, and by summer he was beginning the slow climb back to his old life; he'd even started to run again, slowly, with friends. Cheryl, meantime, had finished her nursing degree and had started work in a shelter-based health clinic run by the Boston Health Care for the Homeless Program, a local nonprofit organization that provides the homeless with access to quality health care.

The couple were getting back to the pleasures of their life when, the following December, an MRI showed that the tumor had returned. Cheryl stopped working to care for Jim during what she calls the "most sacred and intimate time of our marriage. We were with each other 24/7."

By April 1998, Jim's speech was so severely affected that Cheryl could barely understand him. But one Sunday, as she knelt beside the couch to give him some water, he ran his hand through her hair and said clearly, "Cheryl, do you see them? Do you see them? The angels, oh, they're beautiful!"

The next day was Marathon Monday in Boston. After the race, a few of Jim's running buddies stopped by. They told Jim about the race and pinned their marathon medals on his pillow. He died that night, surrounded by family and friends. "It was the best marathon of his life," says Cheryl. "He ran right into the arms of God."

After Jim died, Cheryl lost all zest for life. "How would I ever be excited about anything again?" she asks. "I just couldn't even fathom it. I was crazy about this man. The pain was just excruciating."

She kept working in the clinic, but her heart wasn't in it. Then one day, at a staff meeting, she heard about a street outreach program being created by the group's president, Jim O'Connell, M.D. In Boston, as in many cities, certain homeless adults pose special treatment challenges because they resist shelters and social service programs. So a new street team—made up of Dr. O'Connell, a physician's assistant, two registered nurses, two mental-health clinicians, and a researcher—would go to them, supplying primary care as well as on-the-spot medical treatment.

"It really stirred up a passion within me and made me think, This is what I have to do with my life," Cheryl says. The next day, she went to Dr. O'Connell's office and joined the outreach team.

For the past six years, she has spent her days and often her evenings on the streets of Boston. Cheryl and her usual partner, fellow nurse Sharon Morrison, change dressings, remove sutures, treat skin ailments and body lice, take blood pressure, hand out condoms, and administer pregnancy tests and flu shots. They assess the conditions of patients who might need to get to a hospital, and they make referrals for detox or prenatal care.

Cheryl could easily land a high-paying job at one of Boston's prestigious teaching hospitals or in a private medical practice in comfortable Newton or Wellesley. She doesn't consider that an option. "I don't want to be too hokey about this," she says, "but for me, it's all about looking into somebody's eyes and really trying to figure out what's going on. And knowing that underneath the skin, we're all the same. We all have the same desire to be loved and to be happy."

Cheryl possesses a special gift for her work, says Dr. O'Connell. "These people have lost everything," he says of the homeless. "Real love and caring and giving is something that is denied you when you're out there struggling to survive. Cheryl plugs into that. She understands it."

"Harry!" Cheryl rushes out into the middle of Washington Street, a busy pedestrian thoroughfare. "Harry!" she shouts again, waving down a gray-bearded man wearing a T-shirt and a denim vest—a man all but invisible to the store clerks, secretaries, and executives scurrying to work around him.

"You look great," she says when she finally catches him in a big hug. "You're sober!" When they met, years ago, Harry was sleeping in a stairwell near the North Station subway stop, drinking huge quantities of vodka. Cheryl treated him for "immersion foot": The constant damp of living on the street and wearing the same pair of shoes day after day creates painful sores. Harry was perpetually on the team's "high-risk list"—those with severe substance abuse, mental illness, or multiple chronic illnesses, or who are older and frequently hospitalized.

But in October 2002, Harry, 55, checked himself into detox and got clean. Since then, he has moved into a transitional home in a nearby suburb, started working four days a week cleaning parks and streets, and reconnected with family members. "Look at this: I even got my driver's license—there's my picture," he says proudly.

"That's swell, Harry," says Cheryl.

Harry is one of Cheryl's few success stories. More often, the men and women she and her partner call patients are trapped in a cycle of despair and pain, spending their more lucid moments begging for change from passersby. They'll continue to wind up in emergency rooms because of the stab wounds, burns, and beatings inflicted by other homeless people or by thieves looking for an easy victim. They'll eventually ruin their backs and kidneys sleeping on the cement, suffering dehydration in summer and frostbite in winter. They'll ignore conditions like scabies and lice and tuberculosis until the discomfort becomes too great—and successful treatment uncertain.

Cheryl can be tough if she has to be. When Kevin, a young man who was recently stabbed in the mouth, rails against the system and at Cheryl for being part of it, she says sternly, "We're here to help you. But you have to calm down. If you don't calm down, we're going to leave." But more often, her approach is soothing, even lighthearted. "They know if you're not sincere, and they will call you on it," she says.

One day late last year, as part of her rounds, Cheryl headed toward the New England Holocaust Memorial Park to check on some of her regulars. There she ran into Bobby, a lanky, shirtless man with a skull tattoo on his biceps and a missing front tooth.

Bobby greeted her warmly, handing her a wrapped package that contained an intricately carved wooden box from one of the souvenir shops in nearby Faneuil Hall. He had bought the box with his panhandling money. "I love you," he said, wrapping his long bare arms around her neck.

Later, Cheryl will say that it's her homeless patients' gratitude and trust that keeps her going—that and the belief that she follows a calling.

"It helps me to be able to talk to my patients [like Jack] about what's broken inside and what they are hoping for," she reflects. "I want to provide an opportunity for them to speak about what's important to them."

Cheryl pauses, then adds, "I don't think that most people ever get a chance to do that."[28]

The Best Inspirational Quotes

People who say they sleep like a baby usually
don't have one.

—LEO J. BURKE

Fear and worry are interest paid in advance on
something you may never own.

—ANONYMOUS

Smart is believing half of what you hear; brilliant is
knowing which half to believe.

—ANONYMOUS

Death is more universal than life; every man dies;
not every man lives.

—A. SACHS

Every oak tree started out as a couple of nuts who
stood their ground.

—ANONYMOUS

I try to avoid looking forward or backward, and try
to keep looking upward.

—CHARLOTTE BRONTE

Courage is fear that has said its prayers.

—DOROTHY BERNARD

The Path to Peace

BY JAMES R. ADAIR

"HOW DID A NICE Jewish boy like me end up doing what I do for a living?"

That's how Lon Solomon sometimes begins his story. He is senior pastor of McLean Bible Church in the Virginia suburbs of Washington, D.C., where he ministers to more than 8,000 people each weekend. He is chairman of the executive committee of the Board of Jews for Jesus and was appointed by President George W. Bush to serve as a member of the President's Committee on Mental Retardation (he and his wife Brenda have a special needs daughter, Jill).

Lon points out that he was born into a conservative Jewish home in Portsmouth, Virginia, went to Hebrew school twice a week, and was bar mitzvahed at age 13, "the way every good Jewish boy ought to be," he quips. "I can remember as a little boy trying to talk to God, but I had no connection with Him. I believed God probably existed, that He was out there 'somewhere,'" he says.

When he was 17, a girl in high school asked him if he had assurance that he was going to heaven. She told him if Jesus wasn't his Saviour, he would go to hell. This prompted Lon to question his rabbi. "All Jewish people go to heaven," the rabbi told Lon. "Hell is a Gentile problem. As Abraham's descendants, we have a different kind of arrangement with God than the rest of the world does."

That gave Lon the idea he could do "all kinds of stuff—lie, be nasty—and go to heaven." Years later he ran across Jewish rabbinical writings that actually say this very thing, he recalls.

And for years he did "all kinds of stuff." At the University of North Carolina, excited about having parental constraints removed and remembering what his rabbi had told him, he did more sinning than studying. "I joined a fraternity and you can't imagine all that went on," he tells. "If you saw the movie 'Animal House,' my fraternity made 'Animal House' look like a Christian Day School.

"I got deeply involved in drinking and partying and women and gambling. We would gamble all night. We'd start playing cards around 5 o'clock in the afternoon and gamble all night.

"What about classes? We weren't there for classes; we were there for fun. All you had to do was attend enough classes and maintain a 2.0 grade level to stay out of the Vietnam war and everything was copacetic," Lon explains.

By the beginning of his junior year, the fun of previous years had become stale. "It was kind of 'Been there, done that' type of thing," he recalls. He began asking himself such key questions as "Where am I going?" and "What is life all about?"

In the summer of 1969, while working at a New York resort in the Catskill Mountains, he joined about 500,000 young people at the famous Woodstock Music Festival, and was introduced to LSD. Friends said the drug would "enlighten the mind."

He returned to UNC to start the next year of school, convinced he had discovered the pathway to expand his mind and became a strong pusher of drugs, talking a large percentage of his frat brothers into joining him on that pathway. He dressed the part of a hippie, growing a huge Afro, wearing bell-bottoms and tank tops, motorcycle boots, and love beads. The 1969-70 UNC yearbook inside front cover pictured him and several fraternity brothers sitting in a tree in the middle of the campus smoking dope. "That was life at Chapel Hill," Lon quips.

The turning point in Lon's life began in the spring of 1971. About 2 o'clock one morning he and a frat brother sat on a wall in downtown Chapel Hill, tripped out on LSD, and talking. "You know, David, we're the love children, but instead of getting better, getting more loving and caring, I really feel like I'm getting worse," Lon muttered. David returned, "Maybe not worse, Lon, but getting more honest."

"That hit me like a sledgehammer," Lon recalls. "I had grown up believing my own PR, believing I was a good person, a nice person who was headed for heaven. All of a sudden I was seeing myself as a selfish, self-centered, immoral person in deep and desperate need. I needed to change and decided I needed to find God."

He delved into Eastern religions but couldn't make them work. "I would go out and read Zen Buddhism for the first three hours of the morning, sitting in the woods with my legs crossed, then ask a friend, 'Hey, what's for lunch?' and blow my whole Zen for the day. I thought of joining the Hare Krishnas, except I hated their food. It's awful! I would starve to death! I told myself," Lon continues. "So finally I decided to go back to Judaism."

He visited a rabbi on campus, who gave him some books to read. But he didn't want books.

"I wanted someone to look me in the eye and answer my questions, to tell me how to get changed on the inside and not be that ugly person I knew I was," Lon recounts.

Feeling it was stupid to grow up and live the kind of life he was living, he contemplated suicide. "But I procrastinated in so many things, I just didn't get around to it," Lon says with a chuckle.

Then during that spring of 1971 he met a man, Bob Ekhart, whom he viewed as "the weirdest man in the Universe." Lon's dog, Noah, a German shepherd, got into a little fight with another dog right in front of Bob Ekhart on Main Street. Bob was a man in his forties who drove to Chapel Hill from Durham every Saturday with his wife in a white Econoline van that had Scripture verses written on the sides. He blared hymns from megaphone speakers on top of his van, and, with his wife, handed out Gospel tracts.

Bob helped Lon separate the two dogs. Eye to eye with the "weirdest man in the world," Lon gulped and said, "Hi. Gotta go." As he walked away, something inside said, "Lon, this guy's got peace, the contentment, the wholeness you're looking for."

One Saturday morning Lon walked up to him and said, "I'd like to talk to you sometime." Bob said, "How about 3 o'clock this after-noon?"

Lon wasn't ready for that. So he lied that he had an appointment and said he would see him next week. The disillusioned collegian began walking away down the crowded street, with Bob screaming, "You may not be here next week!" As he thought about it, Lon real-ized he could be dead by then. He had lost two high school friends, one in a motorcycle accident and another had died of a kidney infection.

So at 3 o'clock that same afternoon he showed up to talk with Bob. But he was gone!

"He didn't know I was coming," Lon explains. "The next week was horrible. I stayed off my friend's motorcycle and was careful to look both ways before crossing the street. I didn't walk under any ladders or let a black cat cross my path." He was so scared that he went to a bookstore to buy a Bible but backed out because they were so expensive. Five dollars was all he had.

"On Saturday morning I got up at the crack of dawn, which in those days was about 10 o'clock. And I went downtown to see this guy," Lon recounts. "He takes out a Bible and starts reading from it. He read to me from the Old Testament about Elijah and the prophets on Mt. Carmel. I thought that was the greatest story I'd ever heard! He read from the New Testament about Jesus. I took it in like water on a dry sponge. After about two hours, Bob asked, 'Are you ready to receive Jesus?' I didn't have a clue what that meant, and I responded, 'No, no, no! Jewish people don't do this.'"

Bob countered, "Lon, do you realize that all the early followers of Jesus were Jewish? Everybody who wrote the [words of the] Bible, with the exception of Luke, was Jewish. Would you do me one favor and read the Bible and let God speak to you?" Lon agreed, thinking it would do no harm.

The previous Wednesday Lon had said to God, "If you are real, prove it by giving me a Bible." He felt the odds of someone giving him a Bible were less than zero. Now Bob opened a box and gave him a brand-new Bible!

As Lon walked away, thoughts bombarded his mind: *Could Jesus Christ be the Messiah of Israel? Is what Bob told me true?*

When he began reading the New Testament, Lon was impressed with Jesus. He used words that cut right to the heart of things. He could say more in one sentence than Lon's professors could say in a whole semester, it seemed.

Then he came to Matthew 11:28-30 where Jesus invites those who are burdened down and overwhelmed to come to Him for peace and rest. "This is exactly what I'm looking for," Lon told himself. He got on his knees and prayed sincerely, "God, I don't know if You're real. I'm confused about Jesus. I'm empty on the inside, hurting, lonely, scared. I need some help. . . ."

"It was the worst salvation prayer you ever heard," Lon declares. "I promised to give God my life for a month and see what happened."

Afterward, he got back on his knees to test God. He asked Him to heal his dog of the mange. He had been using medicine, but the disease was getting worse. If his dog got well, he would know God was real. He quit using the medicine, and in a few days the mange was gone.

About a week later he was back on his knees. "God, I'm convinced! You not only healed my dog, but You've changed me on the inside. There's a joy, a peace, and a contentment that I never felt before."

The next Saturday he told his story to Bob Ekhart and his wife. They were thrilled. Later, Bob baptized him in a pond in Chapel Hill.

And that's how Lon Solomon, "a nice Jewish boy," met his Messiah, turned his back on his old life, and headed along a pathway that led him to a large evangelical pulpit.

When Lon told his relatives that he had come to Christ, some were not thrilled. But eventually the members of his entire nuclear family received Christ.

Lon Solomon went on to graduate with highest honors from Capital Bible Seminary (Lanham, Maryland). In 1980 he became senior pastor at McLean Bible Church, which since then has become one of America's thriving mega-churches.[29]

Finding Freedom

BY GRACE FOX

*P*REGNANT—HOW COULD I be so stupid? College junior Francine buried her face in her pillow. *I can't tell Mom and Dad—they would be terribly disappointed in me.* She recalled a friend's predicament a few months earlier and shuddered. *Church gossip will crucify me. What should I do?* she thought.

The college student weighed her options. *Abortion is the only way to fix this,* she thought. Her choice, however, only compounded her problems after she went through with it.

Inner turmoil devastated Francine. Memories haunted her. Bad dreams stalked her sleep. She clutched her secret for three decades, ignoring the pain and fearing what others might think if they knew her past.

Today, popular Christian fiction author Francine Rivers, whose 15 books have sold more than 2 million copies, willingly relates her personal abortion experience. She longs to spare others the heartache she endured. She wants to expose abortion's far-reaching aftermath and bring hope to those suffering its relentless torment.

"For years I carried a heavy burden of guilt, fear, and shame. I lived with a horrible inner cancer. I didn't want to discuss or think about it," Rivers says. "Healing came only after I acknowledged what I had done. I confessed it as sin committed against a holy God and received His forgiveness."

Before she released her burden and found freedom in forgiveness, that inner cancer spread to her marriage. When she married Rick Rivers, a friend since fifth grade, she kept her secret from him. "That was a big mistake," she admits. "When I eventually told him, he felt hurt. He said, 'You didn't trust that I loved you enough.' He was right. Trust is a huge issue for post-abortive women, especially if they were abandoned in their situation."

When Francine miscarried the couple's first child, she blamed herself. *God is punishing me,* she thought. After their second child's birth, she miscarried again. Guilt struck once more. *God, in His wrath, is taking back from me what I took from Him.*

Although Rivers suffered secretly, she appeared strong and ambitious to outsiders. She raised three young children and established herself as a successful secular romance novelist. Although she and her husband were not yet believers, her family attended church faithfully.

But public success and church attendance weren't enough to overcome the struggles. In 1986, with Francine considering divorce, the couple moved to northern California. A little boy welcomed them as they unloaded their van.

"Have I got a church for you!" he exclaimed.

Francine accepted his invitation. "Immediately upon entering the church, I felt like I had come home. This was what I'd been waiting for all my life," she says. "The preaching came straight from God's Word. The people's friendliness drew me in. But there was one problem: Rick was sick of church."

Francine found a compromise. She asked the pastor to lead a

weekly neighborhood Bible study in their home. God's Word filled their hearts, and before long, the couple received Jesus Christ as Saviour. They were later baptized together. God instantly began working in Francine's heart concerning her abortion, gently urging her to face the reality of what she'd done.

"Why are You bringing this up again, God?" she prayed repeatedly. "You've forgiven me. Why must I relive it?"

"Because you haven't given it to Me," God seemed to answer. "I took this burden to the cross 2,000 years ago, but you're still carrying it around. Give Me your load."

Eight years passed, during which Rivers wrote five books for the Christian publishing industry. But her unresolved inner conflict refused to disappear. She cringed whenever she heard the word abortion. A recurring thought terrified her—perhaps God wanted her to write a book addressing the issue. Her other novels flowed from personal struggles. She had written and wrestled through topics such as anger, forgiveness, God's sovereignty, and witnessing to friends who are hostile to the Gospel. As she'd prepared each manuscript, intensive Bible study had deepened her understanding of God's perspective. Why not write about abortion? The characters could represent different viewpoints but Scripture would teach God's thoughts.

No way, Rivers argued. *I don't want to go there. I don't want to write that book. I don't want to think about it anymore.* Several circumstances weakened her resistance.

One day her elementary-aged son, unaware of his mother's past, blurted, "Every woman who has had an abortion should be executed for murder." His comment cut Rivers. *That's what he's learning in a Christian school? Why would any post-abortive woman go to that church for help? We all deserve death. We're all sinners, but for the grace of Jesus*

Christ.

She began examining the church's response to post-abortive women. Too often she sensed a self-righteous attitude, a mindset that cried, "We can't let sinners inside—they might bring a disease!"

This is wrong! Rivers reasoned. *We're to share Christ's love with the lost and hurting and those who have fallen. We're not to close our eyes and ears and doors to them! If post-abortive women can't share their pain within the church, where can they turn?*

Another dilemma bothered her. She became aware of ostensibly Christian institutions expelling pregnant female students. "Even though the school boards weren't saying it, the girls heard the message, 'If you get rid of the baby so no one knows, you may continue your education here.'"

When Rivers discovered that her own mother had hidden an abortion for more than 40 years, she began wondering how many other women had shared the same secret sorrow. "My mother had a late term therapeutic abortion," she says.

"Because she had tuberculosis, doctors and my dad convinced her she would die otherwise. She and my father never spoke about it, until one week before Dad died and he simply said, 'I wonder if we made the right decision.' She wept as she told me that my brother would have been 44 years old if he'd lived. I remember thinking, *Forty-four years and she's still crying—I'm never going to get over my experience. And neither are countless other women.*"

Francine's concerns grew. She could remain silent no longer. In preparation for writing the book, Rivers researched information from a crisis pregnancy center and pursued counselor training. In the process, she admitted her past and expressed her desire to help others in similar circumstances to make life-sparing decisions.

When an instructor counseled her to take the post-abortion classes first, her healing journey began.

Friends prayed for Rivers during her classes. A post-abortive woman now strong in her faith sponsored her, coaching her through the Women in Ramah Bible study. For the first time, Rivers realized she was not alone in her distress. She saw a photo containing numerous white crosses, each one representing 100,000 aborted babies. *And for each baby, there's a suffering mother*, she thought.

Also for the first time, she grieved her lost child, naming him Jedidiah, "beloved of God." In society, women aren't given permission to mourn their aborted children," she says. "They're told to go on with their lives, that they were carrying only fetal tissue, not a child."

Rivers fully acknowledged her actions 30 years previous and acknowledged Christ's forgiveness. "I had head knowledge but not heart knowledge," says Rivers.

"There's a big difference. Head knowledge didn't bring freedom. Heart knowledge made me free to tell others what I'd done and talk about its impact on my life."

As Rivers worked through the post-abortion program, she wrote the book *The Atonement Child*. At its completion, she knew she'd done what God had urged her to do all along—she'd given her burden to Him and found the rest He'd promised (Matt. 11:28-30).

The book has sold more than 168,000 copies. It exposes abortion's ripple-effect on society. Its characters grapple with tough questions that find answers in Scripture. Rivers receives letters from men and women impacted by its message, saying it echoes their experience. "I'm encouraged to know someone else understands my feelings," readers write.

"Thank you for reminding me that God still loves me. He forgives that horrendous thing I did."

Rivers relates her testimony in churches, urging believers to bear the burdens of post-abortive men and women (Gal. 6:2). And she encourages post-abortive men and women to exchange their secret burden for God's peace.

"My freedom came when I admitted, 'This is what I did. This is what it did to my life.' Even though I'd placed my faith in Jesus Christ, years passed before I trusted Him with my private, excruciating pain," she tells the audience.

Scanning the crowd, Rivers notices several women avoiding eye contact with her, their body language communicating their well-kept secret. "God forgives. God restores. But we must give Him our burden. When we grasp the depth of His love and mercy, we experience healing and restoration."[30]

Th Best Inspirational Quotes

A ship in harbour is safe, but that is not
what ships are built for.

—William Shedd

God does not love us because we are valuable.
We are valuable because God loves us.

—Archbishop Fulton J. Sheen

Life is a lot like tennis—the one who can serve best
seldom loses.

—Anonymous

Great men are little men expanded; great lives are
ordinary lives intensified.

—Wilfred A. Peterson

Talk is cheap because supply exceeds demand.

—Anonymous

Do all the good you can, to all the people you can,
in all the ways you can, as often as ever you can,
as long as you can.

—Charles Spurgeon

The mark of a man is how he treats a person who
can be of no possible use to him.

—Anonymous

Faith on the Frontier

REMEMBER A DAY during one winter that stands out like a boulder in my life. The weather was unusually cold, our salary had not been regularly paid, and it did not meet our needs when it was. My husband was away traveling from one district to another much of the time. Our boys were well, but my little Ruth was ailing, and at best, none of us were decently clothed. I patched and repatched, with spirits sinking to their lowest ebb. The water gave out in the well, and the wind blew through the cracks in the floor.

The people in the community were kind and generous, but the settlement was new, and each family was struggling for itself. Little by little, at the time I needed it most, my faith began to waver. Early in life I was taught to take God at His word, and I thought my lesson was well learned. I had lived upon the promises in dark times, until I knew, as David did, "who was my Fortress and Deliverer." Now a daily prayer for forgiveness was all that I could offer.

My husband's overcoat was hardly thick enough for October, and he was often obliged to ride miles to attend some meeting or funeral. Many times our breakfast was Indian cake and a cup of tea without sugar. Christmas was coming; the children always expected their presents. I remember the ice was thick and smooth, and the boys were each craving a pair of skates. Ruth, in some unaccountable way, had taken a fancy that the dolls I had made were no longer suitable; she wanted a nice, large one, and insisted in praying for it. I knew it was impossible; but, oh, how I wanted to give each child a present! It seemed as if God had deserted us, but I did not tell my husband all this. He worked so earnestly and heartily, I supposed him to be as hopeful as ever. I kept the sitting room cheerful with an open fire, and tried to serve our scanty meals as invitingly as I could.

The morning before Christmas, James was called to see a sick man. I put up a piece of bread for his lunch—it was the best I could do—wrapped my plaid shawl around his neck, and then tried to whisper a promise, as I often had, but the words died away upon my lips. I let him go without it. That was a dark, hopeless day. I coaxed the children to bed early, for I could not bear their talk. When Ruth went, I listened to her prayer; she asked for the last time most explicitly for her doll and for skates for her brothers. Her bright face looked so lovely when she whispered, "You know, I think they'll be here early tomorrow morning, Mamma," that I thought I could move heaven and earth to save her from disappointment. I sat down alone, and gave way to the most bitter tears.

Before long James returned, chilled and exhausted. He drew off his boots; the thin stockings slipped off with them, and his feet were red with cold. "I wouldn't treat a dog that way; let alone a faithful servant," I said. Then, as I glanced up and saw the hard lines in his face and the look of despair, it flashed across me, James had let go, too. I brought him a cup of tea, feeling sick and dizzy at the very thought. He took my hand, and we sat for an hour without a word. I wanted to die and meet God, and tell Him His promise wasn't true; my soul was so full of rebellious despair.

There came a sound of bells, a quick stop, and a loud knock at the door. James sprang up to open it. There stood Deacon White. "A box came for you by express just before dark. I brought it around as soon as I could get away. Reckoned it might be for Christmas; at any rate, you shall have it tonight. Here is a turkey my wife asked me to fetch along, and these other things I believe belong to you." There was a basket of potatoes and a bag of flour. Talking all the time, he hurried in the box, and then with a hearty good-night rode away. Still, without speaking, James found a chisel and opened the box. He drew out first a thick red blanket, and we saw that beneath was [a pile] of clothing. It seemed at that moment as if Christ fastened upon me a look of reproach. James sat down and covered his face with his hands.

"I can't touch them," he exclaimed; "I haven't been true, just when God was trying me to see if I could hold out. Do you think I could not see how you were suffering? And I had no word of comfort to offer. I know now how to preach the awfulness of turning away from God."

"James," I said, clinging to him, "don't take it to heart like this. I am to blame; I ought to have helped you. We will ask Him together to forgive us."

"Wait a moment, Dear, I cannot talk now," he replied, then went into another room.

I knelt down and my heart broke; in an instant all the darkness, all the stubbornness rolled away. Jesus seemed to be there with me, but now with the loving word: "Daughter!"

Sweet promises of tenderness and joy flooded my soul. I was so

lost in praise and gratitude that I forgot everything else. I don't
know how long it was before James came back, but I knew he too
had found peace.

"Now, my dear wife," said he, "let us thank God together," and
then he poured out words of praise; Bible words, for nothing else
could express our thanksgiving. It was eleven o'clock on Christmas
Eve, the fire was low, and there sat the great box, and nothing in it
touched but the warm blanket we needed.

We piled some fresh logs onto the fire, lighted two candles, and
began to examine the rest of the box's content. We drew out an
overcoat; I made James try it on—it was just the right size. Then
there was a cloak, and he insisted on seeing me in it. My spirits
always infected him, and we both laughed like foolish children.
There was a warm suit of clothes also, and three pair of woolen
hose. There was a dress for me, and yards of flannel, a pair of over-
shoes for each of us, and in mine was a slip of paper. I have it now
and mean to hand it down to my children. It was Jacob's blessing to
Asher: "Thy shoes shall be iron and brass; and as thy days, so shall
thy strength be" (Deut. 33:25). In the gloves, evidently for James,
the same dear hand had written, "I the Lord thy God will hold thy
right hand, saying unto thee, Fear not; I will help thee" (Isa. 41:13).
It was a wonderful box, and packed with thoughtful care. There
was a suit of clothes for each of the boys, and a little red gown for
Ruth. There were mittens, scarves, and hoods; down in the center,
a box; we opened it, and there was a great wax doll.

I burst into tears again; James wept with me for joy. It was too
much; and then we both exclaimed again, for close behind it came
two pair of skates. There were books for us to read; some of them I
had wished to see; stories for the children to read, aprons and
underclothing, knots of ribbon, a lovely photograph, needles, but-

tons, and thread; actually a muff, and an envelope containing a ten-dollar gold piece. At last we cried over everything we took up.

It was past midnight, and we were faint and exhausted with happiness. I made a cup of tea, cut a fresh loaf of bread, and James boiled some eggs. We drew up the table before the fire; how we enjoyed our supper! And then we sat talking over our life, and how sure a help God always proved. You should have seen the children the next morning; the boys raised a shout at the sight of their skates. Ruth caught up her doll and hugged it tightly without a word; then she went into her room and knelt by her bed. When she came back she whispered to me: "I knew it would be here, Mamma, but I wanted to thank God just the same, you know."

"Look here, my wife, see the difference." We went to the window, and there were the boys out of the house already, and skating on the crust with all their might. My husband and I both tried to return thanks to the church in the East that sent us the box, and have tried to return thanks unto God every day since.

Hard times have come again and again, but we have trusted in Him; dreading nothing so much as a doubt of His protecting care. Over and over again we have seen that, "They that seek the Lord shall not want any good thing" (Ps. 34:10).[31]

Widler's World

BY MARTHA VANCISE

WIDLER, A GANGLY HAITIAN teenager, reached for the small packet that the school director handed him.

"Your sponsor sent this for you," the director said.

Years later, Widler would look back on that moment as the time when his world changed from black and white to color.

Widler's sponsor, Mary Lou Flanagan, was introduced to child sponsorship in the early 1980s. At that time her husband was an instructor and mentor to a talented violinist, Jackson Snyder. Jackson's parents were missionaries who continually invited friends and supporters to visit their ministry, Mission Possible, in Haiti. In 1981 Mary Lou and two teaching colleagues accepted the invitation and flew to Haiti.

Just before going to Haiti Mary Lou read a book on the Christian responsibility to care for the poor and downtrodden. As an elementary school teacher, Mary Lou had taught many poor children and had done what she could to encourage them. Nothing, however, could have prepared her for the needs of the "poor and downtrodden" that she encountered in Haiti.

In Haiti, she saw children bereft of basic necessities for survival.

Although the school year was in progress, children sat listlessly on dirt-packed yards in front of thatched huts or slept on rag heaps beside their working mothers in the markets. Their orange, brittle hair and distended stomachs attested to serious nutritional deficiencies and infection with parasites. Few of the children wore shoes, though sharp rocks, glass, and raw sewage littered the ground and streets. Many toddlers were naked.

At Mission Possible's schools, however, Mary Lou saw hundreds of children dressed in clean uniforms and shoes. Along with learning basic reading, writing, and mathematical skills, they received religious instruction and one hot meal a day. For many, it was their only meal. That one meal, however, made a vast difference in their appearance. Their hair glistened black and shiny and they bubbled with the restless energy of typical elementary students. At recess, they raced and played and returned to their classes sweaty from hard exercise. None of the children showed signs of parasite infestation. Mary Lou saw that through a child sponsorship program, she could bring hope for a better future to thousands of Haitian children. Without hesitation, she started sponsoring a child.

During the next years, Mary Lou sponsored several children. Occasionally she received a letter from a sponsored child, but the Mission Possible sponsorship program was in its early stages and since volunteers handled many office duties, communication between sponsors and children were irregular. In spite of limited direct feedback from her sponsored children, Mary Lou encouraged others to sponsor children.

In 1994, Mary Lou, now retired and also a widow, prayed for direction from the Lord. She found encouragement in Jeremiah's words: "For I know the thoughts that I think toward you, saith the Lord, thoughts of peace, and not of evil, to give you an expected end" (Jer. 29:11). That year events began to unfold that would give hope and a future to both Mary Lou and a Haitian teenager named Widler Germain.

Mary Lou volunteered to work during the winter in the sponsorship program at Mission Possible's headquarters in Florida. She worked daily at the tedious job of punching duplicate copies of the children's letters to their sponsor, grade cards, and biographical information. As she fastened the material in a child's folder and slipped a school photo in the photo sleeve, she often prayed for the student. At least once a year Mary Lou traveled to Haiti to visit her sponsored children and to see those whom she called "the precious little ones" whose photos she had filed.

One day in March of 1994, a student's script-like handwriting made her pause. The student had no sponsor, but had written a letter as a class exercise. The content was typical of most of the letters, but the handwriting had exquisite flourishes. Curious, Mary Lou turned to the back page of the folder and read the student's bio information. According to the record, Widler Germain was 14 years old and had 8 brothers and sisters. Since Mary Lou planned to visit Haiti the next month, she made a copy of the student's letter and planned to visit his school and compliment him on his handwriting.

Mary Lou met Widler and on Sunday morning she asked him to sit beside her in church. "I gave him a stick of gum," she said. "He carefully divided it into three pieces. He gave two pieces to friends seated in front of him and stuck the remaining piece in his mouth."

As the service progressed, Widler motioned to a friend who had found a nub of chalk. The friend handed Widler the chalk and Widler slipped Mary Lou's notebook from her lap. Quickly, he began sketching a plant on the notebook. Mary Lou could not believe the intricate tendrils and shadings of the vine. She realized then that the young man's exquisite handwriting was an expression of strong artistic talent and she requested the privilege of sponsoring Widler.

After Mary Lou returned to the States, she sent Widler a packet of colored-lead pencils. The packet of pencils changed Widler's life. From the black and white world of black lead pencils, stubs of charcoal, and scraps of chalk, Widler moved into a world of delicate pastels.

The next year Mary Lou received letters and a grade card from Widler. Along with the expected material, she received a 32-page theme book filled with drawings of delicate flowers, vines, plants, and birds. From then on she made sure that he had an adequate supply of pencils.

When Widler sent a second theme book the next year with increasingly beautiful artwork, Mary Lou went to an art supplier and asked for help in getting Widler started with canvas and acrylics. On one of her trips to Haiti, she took canvas, stretchers, brushes, and acrylic paints to the talented youth. A few months later he gave her a 20" x 24" painting of a simple village scene. Mary Lou gasped with astonishment. The canvas exploded with a profusion of Caribbean color. He had made the broad leap from sketching single flowers, birds, and plants to painting vibrant scenes.

Mary Lou encouraged Widler to continue his education, but also realized that education would not necessarily assure him of a job or income in Haiti. Widler's brother held an engineering degree from the university in Haiti, but could find work only as a low-salaried teacher. While Widler might be a gifted artist, he would never find a market for his work as long as Haiti's unending political upheaval discouraged tourism and economic growth.

Mary Lou, however, refused to allow hopeless Haitian politics to bury the young man's talent. She arranged for Widler to show his paintings to North Americans who visited Mission Possible in Haiti. They bought a few canvases, which provided some income for Widler's family, but many team members were repeat visitors and had all the Haitian paintings that they wanted.

On her visits to Haiti, Mary Lou photographed Widler's art. She rolled up some of his canvases, tucked them in her suitcase, and took them to the States. In Florida and in Ohio, Mary Lou would haul out the photo albums with the zeal of a grandmother and show off his work. If anyone expressed interest, she always "just happened to have" a couple of his paintings for sale. She opened a bank account for Widler and began depositing money from the sales. She taught him money management and the necessity to return to God a portion of his income and to set aside funds to replenish art supplies. The rest of Widler's income went to Haiti to provide much needed support for his brothers and sisters.

By 1998, Widler's paintings included people and market scenes and variations of color themes. His sales, however, were still limited to visitors at Mission Possible in Haiti, or Mary Lou's direct contacts in Florida and Ohio. To make a living as an artist Widler would need to present his paintings in galleries and at art shows outside Haiti. That would require obtaining a visa.

"I never thought he would get a visa," Mary Lou said. "I figured, though, if this is God's will for Widler, He will work it out." Widler not only obtained a three-month visa in 2000, but in July of 2001 he was granted a five-year visa.

With the possibility of Widler being able to sell his paintings in the United States, Mary Lou, with photo album in hand, approached galleries, libraries, museums, hotels, art festivals, and churches in the Findlay, Ohio, area. She asked that they give Widler an opportunity to display his work. "I was amazed," she said, "of how the Lord used many people to open doors to Widler." When Widler arrived in Ohio, Mary Lou was there to guide him as he began showing his art.

In the Midwest where paintings of covered bridges, creeks, pastures, pastel flowers, and graying barns abound, Widler's paintings stopped people in their tracks. Even children paused to look at brilliant birds tucked into the bright green foliage and the silhouette-faced women with baskets on their heads. When Widler returned home to Haiti, he returned with much needed funds to support his brothers and sisters.

That first summer trek to Ohio has become a yearly event for Widler. Each year his paintings have a broader range of exposure and hang in more prestigious galleries. In the summer of 2003, 32 of Widler's paintings hung in the by-invitation-only ArtSpace, the premier art gallery in West Central Ohio.

Along with encouraging and helping promote Widler's art career, Mary Lou took an avid interest in Widler's character and spiritual development. To Mary Lou's delight, Widler has consistently embraced a "sowing and reaping" attitude toward life. During the summers, he sells paintings in the U.S., but then he returns to Haiti to paint, teach art and English in his brother's 400-student school, and teach evening art classes to 15 young men. He never accepts pay for teaching. At age 24 he has begun the construction of his own home.

Child sponsorship provided hope and a future for both Mary Lou and Widler. "Experiences in another culture broadened my world," Mary Lou says. "I see God's presence everywhere. He is at work in the world outside our familiar homes, families, and churches. Widler is an example of what is waiting to happen if we step out in faith to sponsor a child."[32]

I Never Did Forget You

BY EILEEN CONNELLY

It was two days before New Year's, 1999, and my nursing unit in the veterans hospital in Pittsburgh was closing early. I didn't exactly have exciting plans. Separated from my husband, I lived alone.

Not that I was unhappy: I had a close relationship with my five children, and I enjoyed my job and the people I worked with. This New Year's, I'd planned on having a quiet evening—microwaving a dinner and watching TV. Little did I know how quickly my life was about to change.

When I got home from work, there was a message on my answering machine. It was Ethel, the woman who lived above the funeral home that my parents had once owned. She and I had kept in touch after my parents died. "A man from California is trying to get in touch with you," she said on the machine. "His name is Joe Rowell, and here's his number. . . ."

For my entire adult life, the word California did funny things to my heart. That night was no exception. I dialed the number. "Hello, my name is Eileen. I received a message to call you," I said to the man on the other end of the line. "Oh, thank you for returning my call so promptly," he said in a nervous voice. "I'll get right to the point. My wife is looking for her birth mother." I gasped, and he repeated, "My wife is looking for her birth mother."

During the awkward few moments that followed, Joe and I established that his wife, Shelley, was in all likelihood the daughter I had given up for adoption almost 42 years before. Joe asked if I would like Shelley to call me when she got home. Yes, I told him, struggling to compose myself.

The next hour was a blur. I'd kept this secret from my parents, all but one friend, and, eventually, my kids. I had driven across the country to give birth in anonymity. Suddenly, my past had tracked me down.

The phone rang. Shelley sounded almost apologetic. She explained that the last thing she wanted to do was to intrude on my life, but she wanted to thank me for having her. To his day I have no idea what I said. I'm sure I rambled. I know we talked for a long time. She had quite a surprise for me: She and Joe had six children—my six grandchildren. She'd like to get to know me, and my family, she said, but the decision was up to me.

We said our goodbyes and agreed we'd write to each other, and send pictures. In a daze, I hung up the phone. Then I sat down and began writing, bringing to life memories that had stayed locked inside me all those years.

I was the oldest of three children, raised in a small steel-mill town near Pittsburgh. My parents were caring but strict. After high school, I chose to go to nursing school, but even after passing the state boards, I was not permitted to move out of the family home.

While working at the local veterans hospital, I had a brief relationship with a man that didn't work out. A few months later, I began to suspect I was pregnant. Terrified, I looked in the phone book, found a doctor's office several hours from my hometown, and made an appointment under a fake name. He verified my worst fear: I was going to have a baby—and I was almost five months along. Devastated by the shame this would bring to my family, I left the office and never went back.

Soon it became clear: My parents simply couldn't find out. I did private-duty nursing to save money and tried to act as though nothing had changed. For the next few months, except for going to work, I stayed in my room. I watched my weight, wore bulky sweaters, and learned to hold in my stomach.

Around my seventh month of pregnancy, I knew I couldn't hide my growing size much longer. That's when I gave Bunny a call. Bunny, a nurse who worked with me at the hospital, was single and liked to travel. Without telling her the real reason for the trip (I actually didn't tell her until a few days before the baby was born), I suggested we drive to California for an extended vacation. She loved the idea, and we started making plans. Sensing that I was depressed, my parents thought the trip would lift my spirits. Bunny took a leave of absence from her job, and we left Pittsburgh the second week of February, 1957. To this day, I can remember the feeling of relief as we pulled out of the driveway.

After days of driving, Bunny and I arrived in Hollywood, California, and found a motel that rented by the week. Right away I looked up an adoption agency in the phone book, and I snuck out for an early-morning appointment.

On March 19, four weeks after I'd left Pittsburgh, I went to visit the mission at San Juan Capistrano, some 60 miles south of Los Angeles. I lit a candle and prayed that my baby would always be loved and cared for. Four decades later, I was astonished to learn that all of Shelley's children—my grandchildren—attended that mission's school!

On March 20, 1957, my baby girl was born at St. Anne's, at that time a home and hospital for unwed mothers, where I'd been referred by the adoption agency. I named her Mary Kathleen— Mary in honor of the Blessed Virgin Mary, and Kathleen because I loved the song "I'll Take You Home Again, Kathleen." I glimpsed her for only a few seconds after she was born, afraid to ask if I could hold her, since I was giving her up for adoption.

I stayed at the hospital for three long days, struggling with my emotions. Part of me couldn't imagine telling anyone about my baby; another part wanted desperately to take her home. I never expected to have these feelings. I thought I would deliver, sign some papers, and get on with my life. Now, thinking about giving her up was almost too much to bear. But how could I go home with a child conceived out of wedlock, a single mother in 1957?

In those days it was not unusual for a new mother to remain in the hospital for a week, but I was so nervous about my family learning the truth that I signed myself out against medical advice after 72 hours. Before departing, I filled out a form relinquishing custody of my baby to the agency. Because I was so ambivalent, it was arranged that I'd have six weeks to make my decision final. Shortly afterward, Bunny and I drove home, and we never again discussed what had happened.

Back in Pittsburgh, I resumed work at the veterans hospital. On my day off, I made a trip to a Catholic social service office, where I was supposed to talk to someone about the possibility of keeping my child. I remember walking around town for the longest time, trying to get up the nerve to enter that office, but I was too ashamed. After weeks of agonizing, I told the California agency to continue with the adoption. Slowly, I began rebuilding my life. A little over a year later, I got married; over the next two decades, I raised five children. I never did forget my little girl, but with each passing year, the memories became less vivid.

Until now. On New Year's Day, 1999, I was having a quiet dinner at my brother's house with my daughter Colleen, then 34. In the two days since Shelley's call, I'd thought of nothing else. I left after the meal, wanting to be alone. Sensing something was wrong, Colleen came back to my condo with me. After an hour of small talk, I finally got up the nerve to tell her my secret.

"Colleen," I said softly, "before I knew your father, I had a baby. I wasn't married. Your grandparents never knew, and I gave her up for adoption. Two days ago, she called me." There. The words I thought I'd never be able to say were spoken. My heart felt instantly lighter.

"Mom, that's what you've been trying to tell me?" Colleen was excited. "I have another sister?" She made it easy for me—no guilt, no detailed questions.

It was a week before I received the letter from Shelley that I'd been waiting for. "Dear Eileen," it began. "We can't begin to express our joy in speaking to you today. You were so sweet and honest. We have enclosed several photos of our family. Please feel free to call us at any time. Love, Shelley, Joe, and children."

There were two family pictures on Christmas cards, along with a picture of each child: Joey, now 25; Jason, 23; Stacey, 21; Mandie, 18; Lindsey, 15; and Kahley, 12. Six beautiful children. My grandchildren.

Over the next few weeks, I told the rest of my kids about Shelley. I also confided in my brother Michael and his wife, Carol. My family was shocked at my news but also understanding. As for me, each time I told my story, a weight was lifted.

Shelley and I were anxious for a reunion, and I decided to go to

California in late March. It was difficult to wait, but the three
months helped me work through my emotional highs and lows. I
was happy to rediscover my lost child, but I was also sad. I had
missed her birthdays, her first day of school and first Holy
Communion, her wedding day, and the birth of her children. I
hadn't earned the privilege of being her mother. Not wanting anyone to feel uncomfortable, I eventually suggested that Shelley's children just call me Eileen.

There were more surprises along the way. Shelley sent me a tape
of her earliest weeks—shot by Tonight: America After Dark (a
TV program that evolved into the Tonight Show). Back in 1957,
the show was doing a story on adoptions, and Shelley's adoptive
parents agreed to be interviewed. The segment opened with
Shelley's mom and dad sitting in a room, waiting to see their new
baby for the first time. They were led into another room, where
Shelley was lying on a small bed. I watched a young couple hold
my little girl and promise to love and care for her forever. The host
concluded the show with these words: "There is a saying that an
adopted child is baptized twice, once by the church, and once by
her mother's tears." My mother used to watch the show regularly. It
broke my heart to think that she might have caught a glimpse of
the granddaughter she'd never know.

On March 25, 1999, with my daughters Jackie and Colleen along
for moral support, I got on a plane to Orange County, California.

Shelley, Joe, and their three youngest children were at the gate to
meet us. The kids were blond and beautiful; Shelley looked more
like me than any of my other children did. We hugged tentatively
at first, then I pulled Shelley into my arms and held her close. Back
at her house, she went out of her way to make the three of us feel
at home.

The following morning, we drove to Palos Verdes to meet Shelley's parents, Joy and Tom, and her two younger brothers, Thomas, Jr., and Tracy, both adopted. Everyone couldn't have been more gracious. Shelley's mom had made a collage of baby pictures, and I sped through several scrapbooks, trying to recapture my daughter's life.

Our next stop was St Anne's, where I'd given birth to Shelley. Inside, we met with Rhonda, who'd helped Shelley and Joe in their search for me. Rhonda handed each of us a copy of my original records, and we sat quietly reading the mission's notes about the fragile and frightened 23-year-old woman of 42 years ago.

Our five days in California came to an end, but we agreed to meet again in May. It was clear that there was no way for Shelley and me to make up for the lost years. Still, we knew we could start to build a future. Before I left, Shelley gave me a card.

"You know how it feels," it read, "when you're putting together a jigsaw puzzle and you find . . . the one perfect piece? Take that feeling and multiply it by a lifetime, and you'll know how unbelievable it was for me to find you! You were the missing piece I'd been searching for . . . the one who made my life complete."[33]

The Best Inspirational Quotes

Give your problems to God;
He will be up all night anyway.
—Anonymous

All I have seen teaches me to trust the Creator for all
I have not seen.
—Ralph Waldo Emerson

Truth, like surgery, may hurt but it cures.
—Han Suyin

You don't have to lie awake nights to succeed—just
stay awake days.
—Anonymous

Beware of the half truth. You may have gotten hold
of the wrong half.
—Anonymous

He who accepts evil, without protesting it, is really
cooperating with it.
—Anonymous

Life is what happens to us while we are making
other plans.
—Thomas La Mance

Faith Amid the Flames

BY PETER K. JOHNSON

*T*HE FIRE WAS SPREADING quickly. Already, most of the large home had been swallowed by flames. Inside, where the heat was 10 times that of the hottest summer day, several men were carefully but quickly making their way through the inferno. They had seen situations like this before. They knew it was the kind in which disaster is only a step behind.

"We had fire underneath us, fire on top of us and fire behind us," says Jerry Sillcocks, a New York City firefighter and lieutenant at Engine Company 48 in the Bronx. "My ears were burning and the ceiling temperature was 1,100 degrees."

He was attacking a raging fire in a private house with his hose team when the second floor stairway collapsed under their feet. Tumbling backward through a smoky haze to the first floor, the men picked themselves up, regrouped and continued shooting water on the flames engulfing all three floors.

For members of the New York City Fire Department (FDNY), this was just another typical day. Which is why every time the alarm rings in his firehouse, Jerry Sillcocks prays.

"I don't ever go into a fire before I rely on the Lord," he says. "I pray for the men's safety, and the competence and courage to do the job that I've been entrusted with."

Sillcocks is one of more than 1 million career and volunteer firefighters in the United States who calmly risk their lives every day to save people and protect property. Currently, an average of 100 firefighters are killed and 100,000 are injured per year in the line of duty. Yet they eschew being labeled heroes.

"I'm not a hero," Sillcocks says. "This is my job. How can I say that I'm a hero? It's what I love to do. There is a lot of danger, but we are highly trained. Our training has helped me in life-and-death situations to keep my head."

Firefighters are tough, self-reliant professionals. They bunk together like family and share hearty meals around the firehouse kitchen table.

They stake their lives on one another's skill and bravery. Loyalty prevails. A raucous, prank-loving camaraderie masks their devotion to service and caring attitude. They reflect the Maltese cross—the traditional badge of the firefighter—a symbol of honor and protection. Fighting fires is a team effort.

"To be a firefighter, you got [to have] a desire and a love to help people," says John S. Picarello, of Battalion 21 in Staten Island, New York. "I work with some tough, rough guys, but underneath the whole thing there's a heart."

FDNY currently has 11,000 firefighters. Starting pay is $32,724. The department has 228 firehouses that are home to 203 engine and 143 ladder companies. It covers New York City's five boroughs, which include 321.8 square miles, and responded last year to 51,563 fires.

Teamwork is critical to success. Engine companies pump the water to extinguish fires. Ladder personnel find the fire and search for survivors. Sillcocks' engine company handles from 18 to 25 runs in a 24-hour period.

"We rest," he says. "We never sleep."

He normally works a nine-hour tour and a 15-hour tour back-to-back, gets two days off, and then returns for another double tour, capping off a 48-hour workweek.

Living the Christian life in this close-knit community is no wimpy task. The born-again Christians among them are on the front lines sharing their faith whenever possible. Sillcocks became a Christian in 1986 through the witness of another fireman who never missed a chance to share the gospel.

"Jerry, how are you going to heaven?" his friend had asked.

"Because my mom says I'm a good person," Sillcocks had replied.

After examining the Bible with his friend, Sillcocks was convinced he was a sinner. He asked God for mercy while he lay in bed that night.

Since then the Holy Spirit has sparked a desire in him to share his faith in the firehouse. Sometimes he's razzed and called "Father Jerry" or "Jesus Freak," but he lets it roll off his back. He doesn't curse, tell dirty jokes or go partying with the guys.

Co-workers have tried to shock Sillcocks with foul language and by taping pornographic pictures in his locker.

"I don't take it personally," he says. "I'm a good fireman. And whether I'm a Christian or anything else doesn't make a difference. They may make comments, but on the whole they know my performance, and that keeps the camaraderie together."

Sometimes they listen. Sillcocks shared the gospel with John, a friend who rotated to a firehouse on Staten Island. In June 2001 while on duty at 3 A.M., John prayed with another Christian fireman over the telephone to accept Christ. Three months later John was killed in the collapse of the World Trade Center. "I believe John is in heaven with his Savior, whom he acknowledged before he died," Sillcocks says.

Christian firefighters who talked to *Charisma* say their faith is put into action every day. Warren Haring, a retired supervising fire marshal, says God has protected him numerous times. "You're in God's hands and try to do the best you can and be led by the Holy Spirit," he says.

Picarello is an unusual firefighter. A 17-year veteran of FDNY, he also pastors a thriving Pentecostal church on Staten Island with his wife, Elena. They started the House on the Rock Christian Fellowship in a former dance studio in 1996 with nine people. Today the ministry rents the top floor of a factory building and has 100 members.

A kindly shepherd, Picarello mixes easily with his multiracial congregation. He preaches with gusto, without notes, challenging his flock to a week of prayer and fasting. "We need the power of the Holy Spirit so we can be Jesus to this community," he challenges.

Picarello tells his firehouse buddies: "This ain't your mother's church. It's not orthodox. It's all about Christ."

He admits that it's tough evangelizing co-workers. They hide behind a hard exterior, are mum about spiritual matters and face intense peer pressure.

Yet some have come to him late at night when everyone was asleep, asking, "Is this God thing true?" "Will God help someone like me?" Picarello was blown away when a man known for his jesting bared his soul and confessed, "I'm afraid to die."

New York isn't the only place where God is moving among firefighters. George Rabiela, captain of Tower Ladder 14 on Chicago's west side, was a hard-drinking man until he gave his life to Christ 12 years ago during a Church of God service.

Today he says that he's "not ashamed of the gospel," and an incident in 2002 proved it to his fellow firefighters.

Rabiela was returning to the firehouse with his men after dropping off their ladder truck at a maintenance garage when one of them spotted a minivan that had just crashed into a building. Stopping their vehicle, they found a man slumped over in the front seat.

They called an ambulance and learned he was a driver for a pizza-delivery business. He had been robbed and shot several times.

Rabiela, a Mexican-American, prayed in Spanish for the victim and jumped in the ambulance with him. While racing to the hospital Rabiela prayed with the man to receive Christ as Savior. The man died in the emergency room. Rabiela attended the funeral and followed up with his family.

Jose Medrano, firefigher-paramedic at Station 44 in Duarte, California, is fortunate to work with four born-again believers. They witness many heart-wrenching tragedies, especially when children are hurt or killed.

"Without the Lord it would be very depressing," he says.

Medrano prays for victims and shares his testimony when he can, encouraging believers of all stripes to "be the real deal."

"It's all about Jesus living in you," he says.

Tommy Neiman, firefighter-paramedic with the St. Lucie County Fire District in Fort Pierce, Florida, travels across the country giving his testimony to community groups and in churches. His book, *Sirens for the Cross*, describes on-scene fire and rescue calls.

"I'm sensitive to doors God will open to share His love to victims in crisis," he says. Working an overtime shift at Rescue Station 8, he responded to a call that a young man had jumped from the seventh floor of a condominium building.

He found the despondent victim still alive and sprawled on the pavement. "His mangled legs, from his mid-shin down, were covered with blood," he says.

After providing medical help, Neiman shared the hope of Christ with the young man on the way to the hospital. About two weeks later Neiman prayed with the young man in his hospital room to receive Christ as Lord and Savior.

Firefighters for Christ and Fellowship of Christian Firefighters International are targeting the fire-service community with the gospel.

Founded by John White in Los Angeles in 1976, Firefighters for Christ (FFC) is an all-volunteer group with 8,000 members and more than 60 chapters. It sponsors outreaches and distributes 1 million tapes annually as well as thousands of New Testaments.

"Our mission is encouraging firefighters to live their lives for Jesus Christ," White says. "We want our members to be faithful, and the first to start work and the last to quit."

FFC encourages closet Christians who fear a backlash as a result of sharing their faith. "We go alongside them and give them the courage to stand up for Christ in their firehouses," Sillcocks says.

The Fellowship of Christian Firefighters International (FCFI), based in Fort Collins, Colorado, supports a similar mission with 2,400 members in chapters in the United States, Canada, Mexico, Germany and China.

FCFI and the International Bible Society recently compiled a New Testament titled *Answering the Call* that includes color inserts, study guides, a salvation message, and testimonies from firefighters and EMS workers.

The tragedy of 9/11 has recast the role of firefighters in the national psyche. They are deemed heroes like never before. The sacrifice firefighters make to enter a burning building while civilians rush out reached a new level of awareness in the public mind after 343 FDNY members died saving lives at Ground Zero. It underscored the fact that many others die in the line of duty in every state.

The events of 9/11 also created unprecedented opportunities for Christians within the firefighters' ranks to share the gospel. Sillcocks was asked to pray with 100 men before going to Ground Zero for a search-and-rescue operation.

"I prayed for safety and security and for God to put His blessing over the men that night and to watch over us as we worked," he says. "Everyone wanted to hear the gospel after that. It was an awesome time of witnessing."

Both FFC and FCFI staffed ministry tables around the clock on a side street near Ground Zero. Members distributed tracts and Bibles and prayed with rescue and clean-up personnel.

"That prayer table was anointed by God," Sillcocks says. "Many people came to Christ—cops, firemen, Army personnel and civilians."

FCFI Director Gaius Reynolds notes that "no one refused prayer." Tommy Neiman flew in from Florida to help. He participated in the ceremony at Liberty State Park, presenting urns to victims' families, and shared his testimony on an oldies radio station.

However, the spiritual temperature of firefighters since 9/11 has cooled. Christian firefighters have been knocked for proselytizing and mixing religion with work. Apathy has returned, but FFC and FCFI members aren't backing off.

"Without proselytizing, who is going to hear the gospel of Jesus Christ?" Sillcocks questions. "[We can't stop] sharing the love of Jesus and letting [firefighters] know that they need to hear it. Because if something happens in their life, the next tour we go in, a terrorist incident, a biological incident or nuclear incident, where are they going to be when they stand before God?"[34]

Kristen Stryker: Planting for Others

KRISTEN STRYKER HAS been gardening ever since she could walk. She'd follow her mother Patti around the garden, helping out and munching on vegetables. Little did she know that gardening would be the lead to winning national awards from a major gardening company, the State of Ohio, and the President of the United States.

At 9 years old, like many kids in Canton, Ohio, Kristen joined 4-H and became involved in a gardening project. By the time she was 13 she was involved in the Garden Writers Association's Plant a Row for the Hungry (PAR) program, in which produce is donated locally to alleviate hunger. She coordinated a 40-by-60-foot garden and donated all the produce to the Allegheny Indian Center.

"My grandmother is one-half Native American, so I wanted to share the extra produce with folks at the center," says Kristen. The staff there was thrilled since they rarely received donations of fresh produce.

Kristen next set her sights on another institution: the local youth detention center. "I know what it's like to feel a sense of satisfaction when I plant a seed, see it grow, and harvest the fruits of my work," says Kristen. "I thought that same sense of achievement might help people in prison as well—especially if they knew the produce they were growing was going to needy families," she says. As with the Allegheny Indian Center, there was a personal reason for getting involved with the youth detention facility. "My half-brother spent many years in prison and I thought that if he had had a garden, perhaps he would have felt better about himself and not have been in prison so long," says Kristen.

Her "Help Others to Help Yourself" program has been so popular at the local level that the State of Ohio has initiated the gardening program in all 12 state youth detention centers. Kristen couldn't personally visit all the facilities to help set up the programs so she designed and wrote a how-to gardening manual for each facility. In 2002 the gardens donated more than 2,500 pounds of produce to local food shelves.

Kristen's good works have not gone unnoticed. She was a finalist in the Scotts' "Give Back to Grow" Young Gardener of the Year Award, has received many local awards, and in 2001 she was chosen a winner of President Bush's Community Volunteer Service Award. In 2003 she received the Garden Writer's Plant-A-Row Star Gardener award.

At the young age of 17, Kristen is just getting started. She has been encouraged by the President to spread her prison gardening program nationally. She is in the process of contacting each state's correctional facility to get the programs going. Although college is in her plans for next year, and her interest is in forensic science, you get the feeling Kristen will always be a gardener and will continue helping others.[35]

Once I Was Blind

BY VICKI HUFFMAN

WHAT IF ONE MORNING you woke to find that a thick white fog had enveloped your vision? Would you blame God or vow to continue to serve Him despite your more difficult circumstances? And what if, after you learned to cope as a blind person, God graciously restored your vision? Would your restored sight take your focus off God?

This is the story of a man who once was blind but now can see. It's a story of faith in the dark.

Something Missing

Mike Sullivan grew up in a loving Christian home in Birmingham, Alabama. His mother raised him alone after his father passed away from cancer at the age of 24. After earning a marketing degree from Samford University in Birmingham (where he also met his wife Jan), Mike began working for a large American merchandising corporation. The Sullivans started a family—a son and a daughter—and relocated several times as Mike moved up the corporate ladder.

Even though life was good for Mike and his family, he somehow felt something was missing. At age 30, he found out what it was. After hearing a sermon at a revival, Mike realized that he knew about Jesus Christ intellectually—who He was and what He taught—but he had never really received Christ as his Saviour from the penalty of sin. After he and Jan received Christ and began to truly follow Him, the sense of emptiness went away, replaced by a joyful sense of purpose. "I felt like a hundred pounds of rocks had fallen off my back," he recalls. "I became more involved in my family and my church."

Wanting to serve God to the best of his ability, Mike became licensed for ministry in 1981. The family began taking one to two months off work a year to present the Gospel through a puppet ministry. Their travels took them through much of America and around the world.

Once I Was Blind

With a secure job, a loving wife, two kids in college, and a lay ministry in the Dallas area, Mike Sullivan seemed to have an ideal life. But something happened in 1991 that shook his world to its core. Mike's doctor prescribed a medication to treat an inflammation in his lungs. When his vision began to blur, Mike thought he had reached the age when he needed bifocals. He went to an eye doctor where he received a shocking diagnosis. A reaction to the medication had raised the pressure in Mike's eyes and cut off circulation to his optic nerve. The damage was already done and irreversible. Mike had glaucoma, a condition that can cause total blindness. Within a short time, he woke one morning able to see only a thick white fog. He had lost 95 percent of the vision in both eyes—the equivalent of being able to see only through a pinhole in a piece of paper.

Mike suddenly found himself unable to work and having to rely on his wife to take him anywhere he wanted to go. He spent most of his days lying in bed thinking about the things he used to do that he couldn't do anymore. He recalls, "I was depressed. I was angry. I didn't understand why God would allow that to happen. I thought I was serving Him and doing what He wanted me to do."

Mike's employer gave him a generous early retirement package so that he didn't have financial concerns. But he wasn't ready to retire. After the initial period of depression, Mike realized he had been given a Damascus road type of experience: God had used his blindness to get his attention. "It certainly changed my direction dramatically," he says. "I wanted to be useful, to make my life have an impact doing good for someone else."

Counselors tried to help Mike readjust and find a career he could handle without sight. They recommended teaching. Then Mike began seeking God's counsel. One day while listening to the Bible on tape he heard Proverbs 3:5-6: "Trust in the Lord with all thine heart; and lean not unto thine own understanding. In all thy ways acknowledge him, and he shall direct thy paths." He stopped the tape and said, "I think there's something here for me." He listened to it again and again. He went to sleep repeating it in his mind. "When I woke up the next morning," Mike says, "I realized that God was trying to tell me that He had not changed. The only thing that had changed was my ability to see."

God hadn't changed, but Mike did. "I realized that God was still in control. So I said, 'God, I'm not dead yet. You still have a plan for me. I'm not going to find out what it is by staying in bed. I'm ready to do whatever You want me to do, go wherever You want me to go.'"

Almost immediately his path seemed to be clearer. A local

Christian university called and asked him to teach classes in marketing at night and share his testimony. "It was a mission field. I
taught the principles of marketing and taught that you didn't have
to compromise in order to be successful as a Christian," Mike says.

But Now I See
Convinced that he was able to serve God wherever he was and in
whatever condition he was, Mike was content. His puppet ministry
flourished, as well as a business he started selling drug-prevention
and crime-prevention curriculum for elementary grade students.
He was making three times the money he had in his sighted career.

When his son Chris, a Texas A & M student preparing to serve
in agricultural missions, sought his advice about becoming an
intern with a Christian world-hunger ministry in Ft. Myers,
Florida, Mike agreed to go with him to check it out for a week.
The trip in 1994 convinced Chris to take the internship and
brought with it something unexpected. After getting to know
Mike, the organization's director told him, "We've been praying for
a year for someone to help tell our story. We'd like you to come
work for us."

Mike initially turned down the offer but stayed another week to
learn more about the organization. He became so impressed that
he promised to pray about the position. He recalls, "We had just
built our dream house that we had designed ourselves. We had a
business and a ministry. We wanted to stay in Dallas. But we
prayed about what to do—that God would make it clear so there
would be no question in our minds—and went to sleep."

The next morning a man called and wanted to buy their business. He had seen a newspaper article on Mike's business titled
"Blind man overcomes disability to start over." It was no prank call.

Mike named a price and the man sent a check that morning.

Determined to go if God removed the obstacles, the Sullivans stuck a For Sale sign in the front yard of their dream house. Despite a soft real estate market in the area, the house sold at full asking price in a short period of time.

The Sullivans accepted the job and headed east. Jan was driving near Ocala when Mike suddenly realized he could see more than a pinprick of light. A giant billboard advertising a nightclub was the first thing he made out. Not wanting to alarm Jan he said, "Something has happened to my eyes. I can see more than I'm supposed to." She asked her husband what he could see. He read to her the personalized license plate on the car in front of them: "My T God."

Doctors confirmed that Mike's eyesight had been restored. When Mike tells his story, he compares it to the biblical account of the 10 lepers who asked Jesus to heal them. The Bible says that as they went, they were healed. Mike, too, was restored as he went to do what God had directed him to do. Remarkably, he had accepted his blindness and never prayed to be healed. But with a gracious God such as he serves, Mike has seen how all things are possible.

After he arrived in Florida, Mike got a personalized license plate for the car that he could once again drive. The license plate testifies to what Mike has experienced: there is a "Mi T God."

Mike Sullivan's job involves telling the relief organization's story to groups. Mike has used his story, which he includes now every time he speaks (about 150 times a year). Mike never tells his listeners that his experience was normal or something to be expected. Instead, he encourages people to trust in the grace of God and to realize that no matter what their circumstances—God has a plan for them and can use them despite any limitation.[36]

Open Door, Open Arms

BY GRACE FOX

*T*HE YEAR WAS 1976. Elvira Corben, an emergency room nurse working in Vancouver, British Columbia, comforted a 12-year-old patient being treated for superficial bullet wounds.

Corben's heart broke as she pondered the youngster's situation. The girl had been shot by her mother. Her 14-year-old brother had been killed in the same attack. The mom lay in another hospital room after surviving an unsuccessful suicide attempt.

What would drive a mother to such desperate measures? Corben wondered in astonishment. She knew neither drugs nor alcohol had played a role. It appeared the accused was a single mom who simply couldn't cope with life's pressures.

She's not alone, the Lord seemed to whisper. *There are many women in the same position—alienated, viewed as losers on welfare. They need a place to go for support where they're surrounded by other women, a place where they feel like family.*

Corben took the whisper to heart. By the next morning, she knew that the supportive environment would be her living room. Two friends shared her concern. Together they prayed and set goals: offer friendship to single moms and provide free baby-sitting two mornings each week for their children. After having Corben's home licensed for child care, the women placed a newspaper ad. It read, "Loving Christian women eager to do free child-minding and provide free lunch for single moms." It worked. At times the trio cared for 21 children.

To their amazement, however, the moms chose to stay rather than run errands or enjoy four hours alone. The woman-to-woman interaction proved to be a lifeline for those without close friends or immediate family support.

One year after Corben opened her home, she quit her nursing career to develop the non-profit organization known today as "The Open Door Ministry for Single Moms."

Eventually the need for larger facilities necessitated moving into a church. Presently, five churches in British Columbia offer their buildings as venues for the program. The ministry functions with its own directors. Screened volunteers represent several churches.

The Open Door's ministry remains true to its stated vision: To express Christ's love and His teachings in tangible and practical ways with single mothers and their pre-school children with a view to pointing them toward a personal relationship with God through Jesus Christ.

Besides offering free childcare, lunches, and a caring environment, The Open Door provides a clothing exchange and celebrates participants' birthdays, Mother's Day, Christmas, and Easter. Volunteers often accompany moms to major medical appointments and lend moral support when difficult court cases arise.

Corben also started a catering business that services church functions several times each month. Open Door participants receive $10 per hour, on-the-job training, and references for future work. The ministry helps provide scholarships for moms wishing to return to school.

Spiritual needs are addressed through optional Bible studies. While some moms attend simply for an extra hour of childcare, others are genuinely interested in knowing about God's Word.

"Since we started the Bible study in 1977, I'd say 99 percent of our women have attended it for an extended time," says Corben. "Some have incredibly warped ideas about Christianity, having grown up in Christian homes infiltrated by abuse. They're confused; they have to be retaught. Others have no Bible knowledge at all."

Women stand amazed when they witness answers to prayer. On one occasion, a mom requested prayer that her estranged husband would return her washing machine. He did.

In another instance, The Open Door, which operates by donations, needed $1,500. The volunteers invited the moms to pray with them. The next morning, the first $600 arrived in the mail. Amazed, one mom said, "Wow! God is really faithful!"

During the last quarter century, Corben has witnessed countless single moms receive Christ into their lives. "I've come to understand that we can't untangle these women from their messes," she says. "Only God can, through Jesus Christ."

Sadly, Corben's enthusiasm isn't always reflected in the lives of church-goers who fear their facility will be damaged or cigarette butts will be left behind. "This ministry is about getting into the ditch with people whose lives are a mess," Corben says.

"We model this ministry after Matthew 25:35-40," adds Corben. "Jesus wasn't interested only in a person's soul, although that was the most important thing. He cared about the whole person."

Using the Samaritan woman's example (John 4:4-26), Corben points out that Jesus met people where they hurt. "He didn't wait for the Samaritan woman to come to the temple. He knew she needed water so he went to the well," she says. "These women will never go to church on their own; we have to meet their most desperate need first. That's usually child-minding and friendship. In the process, we offer them the hope Christ offers."

Erica Chamberlain testifies to the truth of Corben's words. Struggling with alcoholism and a crumbling marriage, she became involved with The Open Door.

"The women were there for me when everything in my life fell apart," says Erica. "I don't know if I would have survived that time without their friendship and direction."

Chamberlain says The Open Door is where her spiritual walk began. She recalls making a life-changing phone call after hearing God's Word and experiencing His love through the ministry. "I phoned a volunteer and asked, 'How do I get this God into my life?'" she says. "She explained how to receive Christ into my heart, and I did it."

Corben chuckles when she recalls placing the newspaper ad in 1976. "We didn't have a clue what we were doing," she says, "but God knew. The only thing we knew for certain was that we had to pray, and we did."

God has certainly answered. "When it comes to God changing lives," says Corben, "I've witnessed miracles."[37]

Christmas Love

*T*HIS IS A FIRST-PERSON account from a mother about her family as they ate dinner on Christmas Day in a small restaurant many miles from their home. Nancy, the mother, relates:

We were the only family with children in the restaurant. I sat Erik in a high chair and noticed everyone was quietly eating and talking. Suddenly, Erik squealed with glee and said, "Hi there." He pounded his fat baby hands on the high-chair tray. His eyes were wide with excitement and his mouth was bared in a toothless grin. He wriggled and giggled with merriment.

I looked around and saw the source of his merriment. It was a man with a tattered rag of a coat; dirty, greasy, and worn. His pants were baggy with a zipper at half-mast and his toes poked out of would-be shoes. His shirt was dirty and his hair was uncombed and unwashed. His whiskers were too short to be called a beard and his nose was so varicose it looked like a road map. We were too far from him to smell, but I was sure he stank. His hands waved and flapped on loose wrists. "Hi there, baby; hi there, big boy. I see ya, buster," the man said to Erik. My husband and I exchanged looks, "What do we do?"

Erik continued to laugh and answer, "Hi, hi there." Everyone in the restaurant noticed and looked at us and then at the man, who was creating a nuisance with my beautiful baby. Our meal came and the man began shouting from across the room, "Do ya know patty cake? Do you know peek-a-boo? Hey, look, he knows peek-a-boo."

Nobody thought the old man was cute. He was obviously drunk. My husband and I were embarrassed. We ate in silence; all except for Erik, who was running through his repertoire for the admiring skid-row bum, who in turn reciprocated with his own comments.

We finally got through the meal and headed for the door. My husband went to pay the bill and told me to meet him in the parking lot. The old man sat poised between me and the door. "Lord, just let me out of here before he speaks to me or Erik," I silently prayed.

As I drew closer to the man, I turned my back trying to side-step him and avoid any air he might be breathing. As I did, Erik leaned over my arm, reaching with both arms in a baby's pick-me-up position. Before I could stop him, Erik had propelled himself from my arms to the man's.

Suddenly a very old smelly man and a very young baby were relishing their love relationship.

Erik, in an act of total trust, love, and submission laid his tiny head upon the man's ragged shoulder. The man's eyes closed, and I saw tears hover beneath his lashes. His aged hands full of grime, pain, and hard labor gently, so gently cradled my baby and stroked his back. No two beings have ever loved so deeply for so short a time. I stood awestruck.

The old man rocked and cradled Erik in his arms for a moment, and then his eyes opened and set squarely on mine. He said in a firm commanding voice, "You take care of this baby." Somehow I managed, "I will," from a throat that seemed to contain a stone. He pried Erik from his chest unwillingly, longingly, as though he were in pain. I received my baby, and the man said, "God bless you, ma'am, you've given me my Christmas gift."

I said nothing more than a muttered thanks. With Erik in my arms, I ran for the car. My husband was wondering why I was crying and holding Erik so tightly, and why I was saying, "My God, my God, forgive me."

I had just witnessed Christ's love shown through the innocence of a tiny child who saw no sin, who made no judgment; a child who saw a soul, and a mother who saw a suit of clothes. I was a Christian who was blind, holding a child who was not; it seemed God was asking, "Are you willing to share your son for a moment?" when He had shared His for all eternity.

The ragged old man, unwittingly, had reminded me of an important biblical truth: to enter the Kingdom of God, we must become as little children.[38]

Chang and Tennis, a Match Made in Heaven

BY BRADLEY WINTERTON

*W*HAT ARE WE TO SAY about Michael Chang? Who was that 17-year old David who stood so placidly on Center Court at the French Open in 1989, waiting for Ivan Lendl, the mighty Goliath, to serve? "Watch him when a call goes against him," wrote the Los Angeles Times later that year. "He just bows his head, bounces the ball twice, raises his racket, serves. No outbursts. No shrieks. He never approaches the chair, the neck cords standing out in his throat, his face red, his language X-rated. . . . Michael has had a variety of tennis instructors over the years, but the four he relies on most are Matthew, Mark, Luke and John."

Holding Serve, written with the help of Mike Yorkey, doesn't provide any answers to the enigma. But what it does is remind us that humanity is a strange species, and there are more kinds of beings walking this earth than we might sometimes care to think. Michael Chang was, at 15, the youngest player ever to compete in Wimbledon. He was the youngest player ever to win a Grand Slam title. But that famous 1989 French Open has turned out to be the only Grand Slam he's ever won. It's as if he was born to be the boy David, and life's later conquests have somehow partially eluded him.

Consider this. When he traveled to distant championships in those early days, his mom went with him. They shared the same hotel room (to save on expenses), and she would cook up chicken noodles in the rice-cooker she always brought with her. Michael had a huge appetite, though he couldn't put on weight however hard he tried. He describes the night before the 1989 French Open final as follows: "That evening about 10 p.m., as Mom and I prepared to turn out the lights and go to sleep, I took out my New International Version Student Bible. I was in the habit of ending each day with 15 minutes of Bible reading. I liked to learn more about God and how much He loves us."

He reads King Solomon's Proverbs and in saying his prayers remembers "the Chinese people during the difficult time following the tragedy of Tiananmen Square" (which had occurred only days before). His final words are, "Goodnight, Mommy."

But the huge, the enormous paradox is that this pious middle-class son of Chinese immigrants, raised on the public courts of Southern California, won the French Open for the US after 494 other Americans—some of them, no doubt, beer-swilling, loud-mouthed, sexually voracious—had failed. No American male had managed to win the championship, played on its infamous red clay courts, since 1955, 24 years earlier. And who won? A 17-year old Christian, with eyes only for his Mommy with her chicken noodles, and his Student Bible. Even the name is significant. He's not Mike Chang or Mick Chang. He's Michael. And there he stands, waiting to receive serve, patient, unruffled, unperturbed, and ultimately, it would seem, inscrutable.

Sex is at the heart of it, of course, or rather the lack of it. What makes this boy tick, you ask, when he's so different from your average tough-guy sportsman, yet managed to beat them all at their own game? Michael Chang is disarmingly open about it in his book. He's still a virgin at 31, he writes, and saving himself for his eventual wife. She'll be of Chinese origin, he thinks, probably a Chinese American, and she'll be a Christian like him. Then on their wedding night, he'll give her what will be hers alone, a gift no other woman on earth has ever known. So in the mean time Michael lives in his lake-side home outside Seattle, driving his boat to where he most likes to fish, reading his Bible, and wondering what to do now that his tennis career is coming to a close.

Something for God, he thinks. Impressing the young with his extraordinary tennis prowess and celebrity, you imagine, and at the same time suggesting they come along with him to the church to pray. Possibly, he speculates, in China.

As he comes over in this unassuming book, Michael Chang is innocence personified. He wasn't a high achiever at school, and he accepts life and the world in ways that his smarter contemporaries might bridle at.

Even money doesn't appear to bother him much, though his winner's check for US $291,752 in Paris in 1989 more than doubled his career earnings isn't surprising for a 17-year-old. He just thanks God for all his blessings in his prayers every night, after he's prayed for his mom and his family. He never asks God to let him win, though. God has his plans, knows what's best for him and for the world, and Michael doesn't presume to ask him to change them. Michael Chang is a distinctly American phenomenon.

D.H. Lawrence, writing in *Studies in Classic American Literature* considered America a place of innocence, but an innocence the world needed to renew itself. Lawrence himself moved to New Mexico for just that input, just that inspiration. Europe was over-sophisticated and tired, he thought. New things wouldn't come from there. And Bible-reading Christianity is part of that American innocence. In France religious belief has long been associated with ultra-right wing politics. After cheering him following his victory over Lendl, his French fans turned to jeering when he attributed his victory to Jesus.

In the last analysis, Chang reminds us that the usual stereotypes don't account for all people. The teenager who lobbed an underarm serve to Lendl at a crucial juncture, so unnerving him that he went on to lose the point, had no smart plan. "I never thought twice about it," he writes. "I just did it."

Life, then, is a mystery—or, if you prefer, a miracle. Michael Chang has an inner steadfastness, both as a tennis-player and as a man, that other people's incomprehension, and even hostility, can't even begin to shake.[39]

The Moral of the Story . . .

Uncommon Perseverance

Helping the deaf to communicate was Alexander Graham Bell's motivation for his life's work, perhaps because his mother and wife were both deaf. "If I can make a deaf-mute talk," Bell said, "I can make metal talk." For five frustrating and impoverished years, he experimented with a variety of materials in an effort to make a metal disk that, vibrating in response to sound, could reproduce those sounds and send them over an electrified wire.

During a visit to Washington D.C., he called on Joseph Henry, a scientist who was a pioneer in research related to electricity. He presented his ideas to him and asked his advice: Should he let someone else perfect the telephone or should he do it himself? Henry encouraged him to do it himself, even though Bell complained that he lacked the necessary knowledge of electricity. Henry's brief solution was, "If you don't have it, get it."

So Bell studied electricity. A year later, while obtaining a patent for the telephone, the officials in the patent office credited him with knowing more about electricity than all the other inventors of his day combined.

Hard work. Study. Hope. Persistence. These are all "common things." They are also the keys to doing uncommonly well.[40]

❦

THE SECRET OF SUCCESS IS
TO DO THE COMMON THINGS
UNCOMMONLY WELL.

John D. Rockefeller Jr.

Unexpected Genius

Theodor was an artist, of sorts. He drew cartoons for a "creature-of-the-month" ad campaign for a popular insecticide called "Flit." Theodor, however, wanted to expand the scope of his commercial illustrating. Unfortunately, his advertising contract wouldn't allow it, forcing him to try his hand at writing and illustrating children's books.

After twenty-seven rejections of his first attempt, *A Story No One Can Beat*, Theodor was ready to give up. On his way home to burn his manuscript, Theodor ran into an old schoolmate who had just been hired as a children's book editor at Vanguard Press. With a change of the title to *And To Think It Began on Mulberry Street*, Theodor's first book finally made it to press.

Thus began the career of the best-selling children's author of all time, Theodor Seuss Geisel. In addition to winning the Pulitzer Prize for fiction in 1984, "Dr. Seuss" was also awarded eight honorary degrees. When he died at the age of eighty-seven, Theodor's books had sold more than 200 million copies, and he was receiving nearly 1,500 fan letters a week.

How soon is too soon to give up? It is any time before you're absolutely certain God wants you to head in a new direction. After all, who knows what unexpected rewards the second try, the tenth, or the twenty-seventh will hold?

NEVER THINK THAT GOD'S DELAYS ARE
GOD'S DENIALS. HOLD ON; HOLD FAST;
HOLD OUT. PATIENCE IS GENIUS.

Comte Georges-Louis Leclerc Ce Buffon

It's Only Natural

The restaurant was almost empty. Still, the waiter seated Lisa and her grandmother right next to a single businessman, who was enjoying his newspaper and a leisurely lunch. Lisa began to panic. She was accustomed to her grandmother's idiosyncrasies since the onset of Alzheimer's, but she wasn't sure the businessman would be as understanding.

As soon as they were seated, the questions began. "How am I going to pay for this food? I don't have any money. Who's paying my bills? I shouldn't have moved here. I'm just a burden. Why don't you leave me in the gutter to die?"

Patiently, Lisa tried to calm her grandmother's fears, answering the same questions she answered week after week. Forty minutes passed. Lisa couldn't stop worrying about the man sitting next to them. He's trying to relax, she thought. My grandmother's probably driving him crazy.

Lisa was relieved when the man finally folded his paper and prepared to leave. Then to her surprise, he headed straight for their table. Lisa prepared to apologize for any aggravation her grandmother might have caused him. Instead, he looked at Lisa with a smile and whispered, "When I get older, I hope I have a granddaughter just like you."

Even the smallest gesture of kindness can make a big difference in someone's life. Keep your eyes and heart open for the opportunities today brings.

⚬❧⚬

**DO ALL THE GOOD YOU CAN TO ALL
THE PEOPLE YOU CAN, IN ALL THE
WAYS YOU CAN, AS OFTEN AS EVER
YOU CAN, AS LONG AS YOU CAN.**

Charles Haddon Spureon

Championship Character

None of the kids on the block knew why Mrs. Greer was so mean. All they knew for sure was that she hated kids. If a ball rolled into her yard, they forgot it. After knocking on her door once, no one ever tried it again. One day, out of spite, the elderly woman turned on her sprinkler. Instead of watering her front lawn, it was set to water the sidewalk, preventing the children from even riding their bikes in front of her house.

Not being old enough to cross the street on their own, one of their favorite pastimes came to a standstill. Then a smile spread across one child's face, and as he whispered his idea to the others, smiles spread throughout the group. Each kid ran home with a mission. On that sunny, cloudless day the children returned with their bikes—and their raincoats. Their bike ride became a wet and wild adventure, as they rode through the sprinklers, laughing harder than they had with their original game.

When you are faced with difficult circumstances, the decision is yours. You can let a seed of bitterness rob you of joy, like it did the old woman; or you can let circumstances stretch your creativity and lead you in a new direction. Who knows, you may find yourself somewhere you never expected, grateful for the new opportunity.

IF YOU CAN'T CHANGE YOUR CIRCUMSTANCES, CHANGE THE WAY YOU RESPOND TO THEM.

Anonymous

See the Rosy Side

A small dog was struck by a car and tossed onto the shoulder of the road. A doctor, who just happened to be driving by, noticed that the dog was still alive, stopped his car, picked it up, and took it home with him. When the doctor had an opportunity to examine the dog closely, he found that it had suffered only minor cuts and abrasions. He cleaned its wounds and carried it to the garage, where he intended to provide a temporary bed.

The dog, however, wriggled free from his arms, jumped to the ground, and scampered off. "What an ungrateful dog," the doctor said to himself. He was glad that the dog had recovered so quickly but a little miffed that it had shown so little appreciation for his expert care.

The doctor thought no more about the incident until the next evening, when he heard a scratching at his front door. He opened the door to find that the little dog had returned with another injured dog at its side!

Be encouraged! You may never see the difference you make in someone's life or the difference that person will make in the lives of others, but those with whom you share God's love will never be the same.

⚬❧⚬

A CHRISTIAN MUST KEEP THE FAITH, BUT NOT TO HIMSELF.

Anonymous

Just Do It

A young attorney, just out of law school and beginning his first day on the job, sat down in the comfort of his brand-new office with a great sigh of satisfaction. He had worked long and hard for the opportunity to savor such a moment. Then, noticing a prospective client coming toward his door, he tried to look busy and energetic.

Opening his legal pad and uncapping his pen, he picked up the telephone, and cradling it under his chin, began to write furiously. "Look, Harry, about that amalgamation deal," he said to an empty phone line. "I think I better run down to the factory and handle it personally. Yes. No. I don't think three million dollars will swing it. We should have Smith from LA meet us there. Okay. Get back to me."

Hanging up the phone, he put down his pen, looked up at his visitor, stood, extended his hand, and said in his most polite but confident attorney's voice, "Good morning. How might I help you?" The prospective client replied, "Actually, I'm just here to hook up your phone."

There's an old saying that goes, "A shut mouth gathers no foot." Sometimes the best thing to do is just keep your mouth shut!

**I HAVE NEVER BEEN HURT
BY ANYTHING I DIDN'T SAY.**

Calvin Coolidge

Repent!

One day, in the fall of 1894, Guglielmo retreated to his room on the third floor of his parents' home. He had just spent his entire summer vacation reading books and filling notebooks with squiggly diagrams. Now the time had come to work.

He rose early every morning. He worked all day and long into the night, to the point that his mother became alarmed. He had never been a robust person, but now he was appallingly thin. His face was drawn, and his eyes were often glazed over with fatigue.

Finally, the day came when he announced his instruments were ready. He invited the family to his room, and pushing a button, he succeeded in ringing a bell on the first floor! While his mother was amazed, his father was not. He saw no use in being able to send a signal so short a distance. So Guglielmo labored on. Little by little, he made changes in his invention so he could send a signal from one hill to the next, and then beyond the hill. Eventually, his invention was perfected, partly by inspiration, but mostly by perseverance.

Guglielmo Marconi eventually was hailed as the inventor of wireless telegraphy—the forerunner of the radio. He not only received a Nobel prize in physics for his efforts, but also a seat in the Italian senate and many honorary degrees and titles.

You can accomplish anything you set your heart on by combining your vision with hard work.

⌒✣⌒

**THE WAY TO GET TO THE TOP
IS TO GET OFF YOUR BOTTOM.**

Dr. Eugene Swearinger

Your Best Shot

Joe Smith was a loyal carpenter who worked almost two decades for a successful contractor. The contractor called him into his office one day and said, "Joe, I'm putting you in charge of the next house we build. I want you to order all the materials and oversee the job from the ground up."

Joe accepted the assignment with great enthusiasm. He studied the blueprints and checked every measurement and specification. Suddenly, he had a thought. If I'm really in charge, why couldn't I cut a few corners, use less expensive materials, and put the extra money in my pocket? Who will know? Once the house is painted, it will look great.

So Joe set about his scheme. He ordered second-grade lumber and inexpensive concrete, put in cheap wiring, and cut every corner he could. When the home was finished, the contractor came to see it.

"What a fine job you've done!" he said. "You've been such a faithful carpenter to me all these years that I've decided to show you my gratitude by giving you a gift—this house."

Build well today. You will have to live with the character and reputation you construct.

YOU ARE ONLY WHAT YOU ARE WHEN
NO ONE IS LOOKING.

Robert C. Edward

Irregular Role

A band of minstrels from a faraway land traveled about singing and playing their music in hopes of making a living, but they had not been doing well. Times were hard, and the common people had little money to spend on concerts, even though their fee was small.

The group met one evening to discuss their plight. "I see no reason for opening tonight," one said. "It's snowing, and no one will come out on a night like this." Another said, "I agree. Last night we performed for just a handful. Even fewer will come tonight."

The leader of the troupe responded, "I know you are discouraged. I am too, but we have a responsibility to those who might come. We will go on, and we will do the best job we possibly can. It is not the fault of those who come that others do not. They should not be punished with less than our best."

Heartened by his words, the minstrels gave their best performance ever. After the show, the old man called his troupe to him again. In his hand was a note handed to him by one of the audience members just before the doors closed behind him. Slowly the man read, "Thank you for a beautiful performance." It was signed simply, "Your King."

Even if no one else notices the quality of your work, God does. Do your best. Do it for Him!

EVERY JOB IS A SELF-PORTRAIT OF THE
PERSON WHO DOES IT. AUTOGRAPH
YOUR WORK WITH EXCELLENCE.

Anonymous

Unwrap the Gift

During a prayer meeting one night, an elderly woman pleaded, "It really doesn't matter what You do with us, Lord, just have Your way with our lives." Adelaide Pollard, a rather well-known itinerant Bible teacher, overheard her prayer. At the time, she was deeply discouraged because she had been unable to raise the money she needed to go to Africa for missionary service. She was moved by this woman's sincere request of God, and when she went home that evening, she meditated on Jeremiah 18:3-4: Then I went down to the potter's house, and, behold, he wrought a work on the wheels. And the vessel that he made of clay was marred in the hand of the potter: so he made it again another vessel, as seemed good to the potter to make it.

Before retiring, Adelaide took pen in hand and wrote in hymn form her own prayer:

Have Thine own way, Lord! Have Thine own way!

Thou art the potter, I am the clay.

Mold me and make me after Thy will,

While I am waiting, yielded and still.

The best way to discover the purpose for your life is to give yourself, along with all your plans and dreams, to God. Then He can reveal and fulfill His plan for you. You won't be disappointed.

DON'T ASK GOD FOR WHAT YOU
THINK IS GOOD; ASK HIM FOR WHAT
HE THINKS IS GOOD FOR YOU.

Anonymous

I Wish . . .

In 1970, Wally started baking chocolate chip cookies for his friends, using a recipe and procedure that had been passed down from his Aunt Della. For five years he gave away every batch he made, even though people often told him his cookies were so good he should go into business. Wally had other ideas though. He was determined to become a big-time show business manager.

Then one day a friend, B. J. Gilmore, told him that she had a friend who could put up the money for a cookie-making business. Her friend never made the investment, but Wally got some of his own friends—including Jeff Wall, Helen Reddy, and Marvin Gaye—to invest some money. Then he was off and running.

Originally, he intended to open only one store on Sunset Boulevard, just enough to "make a living." After all, his was the only store in the world dedicated to the sale of nothing but chocolate chip cookies. Business grew virtually overnight. Wally's "Famous Amos Chocolate Chip Cookies" were soon distributed worldwide. Wally himself became a spokesman for other products, from eggs to airlines, to a telephone company. While he once dreamed of managing stars, he is now one in his own right!

Sometimes dreams come through the back door. Keep it unlocked!

OPPORTUNITIES ARE SELDOM LABELED.

John A. Shedd

Laughter is the Best Medicine

When Ryan found out his dog, Mulder, was going to have puppies, every morning was a race to the laundry room to see if the miracle had occurred while he slept. One morning, Ryan was rewarded by the sight of nine squirming balls of fur. Knowing that his parents had said he could keep only one, Ryan made the difficult choice of deciding which one would stay and which ones would be given away.

Six weeks later, Ryan made a cardboard sign that he carefully attached to the mailbox in front of his house. It read, "Cute puppies. FREE!" After several weeks, only two of the puppies had been given away, so Ryan decided to try a new approach. His new sign read, "Five cute puppies and only one really ugly one. Free to a good home!" The puppies were gone within the day. Every person who knocked on the door wanted to come to the rescue of that one poor, ugly pup.

Plenty of people want to help the underdog. Too often they're just not sure of how to go about it. Who has God put in your life that could use your help today? It could be a gift of time, finances, elbow grease, or maybe just friendship. Reaching out to help someone doesn't deplete your resources. It actually enlarges your capacity to care.

**THE CAPACITY TO CARE GIVES
LIFE ITS DEEPEST SIGNIFICANCE.**

Pablo Casals

Press On

A story is told of identical twins: one a hope-filled optimist who often said, "Everything is coming up roses," and the other, a sad and hopeless pessimist who continually expected the worst to happen. The concerned parents of the twins brought them to a psychologist in the hope that he might be able to help them balance the boys' personalities.

The psychologist suggested that on the twins' next birthday, the parents put them in separate rooms to open their gifts. "Give the pessimist the best toys you can afford," the psychologist said, "and give the optimist a box of manure." The parents did as he had suggested.

When they peeked in on the pessimistic twin, they heard him complaining, "I don't like the color of this toy. I'll bet this toy will break! I don't like to play this game. I know someone who has a bigger toy than this!"

Tiptoeing across the corridor, the parents peeked in and saw their optimistic son gleefully throwing manure up in the air. He was giggling as he said, "You can't fool me! Where there's this much manure, there's gotta be a pony!"

How are you looking at life today? As an accident waiting to happen, or a blessing about to be received?

THE HAPPIEST PEOPLE DON'T
NECESSARILY HAVE THE BEST OF
EVERYTHING. THEY JUST MAKE THE
BEST OF EVERYTHING.

Anonymous

Peanuts

Harry Houdini, who won fame as an escape artist early in the twentieth century, issued a challenge wherever he went. He claimed he could be locked in any jail cell in the country and set himself free within minutes. Indeed, he made good on this claim in every city he visited.

One time, however, something seemed to go wrong. Houdini entered a jail cell in his street clothes. The heavy metal doors clanged shut behind him, and he took from his belt a concealed piece of strong, but flexible metal. He set to work on the lock to his cell, but soon realized something was wrong. He worked for thirty minutes without success. An hour passed. This was much longer than it usually took to free himself. Houdini began to sweat and pant in exasperation. Still, he could not pick the lock.

Finally, after laboring for two hours, frustrated and barely fending off a sense of failure, Houdini leaned against the door. To his amazement, it swung open! It had never been locked in the first place!

How many times are challenges impossible simply because we think they are? When we focus our minds and energy on them and strike the word "can't" from our vocabulary, impossible tasks are almost always transformed into attainable goals.

CLEAR YOUR MIND OF CAN'T.

Samuel Johnson

Free Indeed

Grace Hopper was born with a desire to discover how things worked. At age seven, her curiosity led her to dismantle every clock in her childhood home! When she grew up, she eventually completed a doctorate in mathematics at Yale University. During World War II, Grace joined the navy and was assigned to the navy's computation project at Harvard University. There she met "Harvard Mark I," the first fully-functional, digital computing machine.

Unlike the clocks in her childhood home, "Harvard Mark I" had 750,000 parts and 500 miles of wire! While most experts believed computers were too complicated and expensive for anyone but highly trained scientists to use, Grace thought otherwise. Her goal was to understand how computers work and then to simplify the intimidating processes so more people could use them. Her work gave rise to the programming language COBOL.

As late as 1963, each large computer had its own unique master language. Grace became an advocate for a universally-accepted language. She had the audacity to envision a day when computers would be small enough to sit on a desk, more powerful than "Harvard Mark I," and useful in offices, schools, and homes. At the age of seventy-nine, she retired from the U.S. Navy with a rank of rear admiral. More important to her, however, she had lived to see her dream of personal computers come true!

Believe in your dreams. With God, all things are possible.

***

THE FUTURE BELONGS TO THOSE WHO BELIEVE IN THE BEAUTY OF THEIR DREAMS.

Eleanor Roosevelt

Heroic Effort

Carrying her bucket of popcorn, Diane hurried into the theater. As the lights dimmed, she carefully climbed over feet, purses, and discarded candy wrappers toward an empty seat in the fifth row. "Just in time!" whispered to an elderly gentleman seated to her left. Even in the darkness, Diane could see the expression on his face was a kind one.

As the movie began, Diane grabbed a handful of popcorn. The man next to her smiled, then put his hand into the bucket, helping himself. Not wanting to cause a scene, Diane ignored him. Perhaps he was senile, she thought. Throughout the movie, Diane ate her popcorn, while the stranger continued to do the same. With one small handful of popcorn remaining, the man tilted the bucket her way, offering Diane what was left. She grabbed it, fuming inside over the man's brazenness.

When the movie ended, the man smiled once more, picked up the empty popcorn bucket, and headed out of the theater. As Diane reached for her purse, she discovered a full bucket of popcorn on the floor next to her. She'd been eating out of the man's bucket the entire time!

It's the size of your heart, not your income, that determines how easily you share with others. Is there anything holding you back from being more generous with what God's given you?

ONE OF LIFE'S GREAT RULES
IS THIS: THE MORE YOU GIVE, THE
MORE YOU GET.

William H. Danforth

Good Connection

Okay, God," prayed Becky. "This afternoon is set aside for you. I'm taking the next two hours just to pray." Becky had never talked to God that long before. Feeling that it might become difficult to stay with it, she wrote out an extensive list of people and problems she felt she needed to pray about.

Soon after she started, Becky felt that she should give her friend Teri a call. She'd wanted to invite Teri and her family over to lunch, but had never quite gotten around to asking them. Fearing that her mind was starting to wander, Becky tried to go back to her list, but Teri kept coming to mind. After several attempts to get her mind back on what she was doing, Becky gave up and phoned Teri.

As Becky began to voice her invitation, Teri started laughing. Taken aback, Becky wondered what great social blunder she had just committed. Teri explained, "Just five minutes ago, I was having a regular pity party, crying because no one at our church ever invites us over. I had just said those very words to my husband when the phone rang."

Are you willing to let God change your agenda? His timing is always perfect. Today when you pray, be sure to listen for God's voice speaking to your heart even as you verbalize your concerns to Him. Why settle for a monologue when you can enjoy a two-way conversation.

❧

**BLESSED IS THE MAN WHO FINDS OUT
WHICH WAY GOD IS MOVING AND
THEN GETS GOING IN THE
SAME DIRECTION.**

Anonymous

The End of the Story, Sort of...

ONCE A YEAR WE CELEBRATE the anniversary of our birth. Even if others forget our special day, it's not a date that slips our own minds too easily. But there is another anniversary that passes by each year unnoticed. That is the anniversary of the day we will die. Though the date remains a mystery, except to God, how we view that day plays a part in how we live our lives.

Would knowing that date change how you spend today? If you knew you still had fifty years ahead of you, would you relax a bit more? Or would you work harder than ever, trying to save enough money to help you make it financially? Would you take those piano lessons you've always wanted? Or would you put them off, knowing you've still got time?

And what if you discovered that the date of your death was tomorrow? Chances are you wouldn't spend today at the office or cleaning house. You'd leave your To Do list unfinished, the dishes unwashed, and gather all the people you love around you to tell them how much they mean to you. You'd savor the beauty of the sunset. You'd enjoy the taste of each meal. You'd be more aware of the passage of time. You'd make every minute count.

Tomorrow may be the day. But then again, you may have fifty years. To be lost in either extreme is to lose sight of the whole story. The key is to learn to live a life that balances both possibilities at the same time. Seize today, while planning for tomorrow. But don't let death convince you it's the final chapter. God isn't finished with you yet...

Though your story on earth may have ended, eternity has just begun. Though what it will really be like is still a mystery, there are clues. God has promised not once, not twice, but three times (Isaiah 65:17, 2 Peter 3:13, and Revelations 21:1) that there will be a "new heaven and a new earth." To me, that's synonymous with adventure. If God's first Grand Canyon was merely grand, imagine what He could do the second time around!

God has also said we'll be given new bodies (1 Corinthians 15:51-52). The blind will see. The lame will walk. The tone deaf will sing. The uncoordinated will dance. We'll have bodies that will work all the time—ones that will never grow old and die, ones we'll not need to compare to those around us.

Best of all, there will be relationship. After all, relationship is the ultimate story. It is never static. In relationship there is growth and change and love and discovery. But in heaven, God has also promised there will be no more tears. (See Revelation 7:17 and 21:4.) Can you imagine the joy of being in a relationship that never gives you cause to cry? A relationship where there is always more than enough time to get to know each other better?

There's only one catch. To experience all of these wonders God has planned for us in heaven, we first must have a personal relationship with Him. How do you begin a relationship with God? There is only one way. Your relationship with the living God, who loves you, begins the moment you receive His Son, Jesus Christ, into your heart and life as your Lord and Savior. The Bible says, "As many as received Him, to them He gave the right to become children of God, *even* to those who believe in His name" (John 1:12 NAS). And Jesus said, "Behold, I stand at the door and knock; if anyone hears My voice and opens the door, I will come in to him..." (Rev. 3:20 NAS). So, why not begin that relationship right now by calling out to Him and inviting Him into your life?

The relationship that you begin on earth with God is just a prelude—the "foreword" of your life's story, so to speak. Though it seems brief in light of eternity, there is something about our lives here on earth that matters deeply to God, and should to us, as well. Everything we do and say either draws us closer to God and others or further away from them. Our actions either bless others or hurt them. They either perfect us or degrade us. While each of us is a work in progress who still blows it along the way, maturing means learning from our mistakes—and letting God change us from the inside out.

Heaven truly is something worth looking forward to. And death, while unsettling in its unpredictability, is not to be feared. God is there. From the first spark of life in your mother's womb, through the mystery of death and into the never-ending story of eternity, you're never alone. God is beside you, loving you and helping you grow. So be patient with yourself and others. God not only isn't finished with us yet. The truth is, He never will be.[41]

ENDNOTES

1. Marti Attoun, "The Woman Who Loved Children," *Ladies' Home Journal*, December 2003, 94-105.

2. Based on "Bethany Hamilton: More Than a Conqueror" by Zsa Zsa Palagyi, http://www.cbn.com/living/amazingstories/BethanyHamilton; "Faith-driven Bethany Holds Her Family Together" by Jan TenBruggencate, http://the.honoluluadvertiser.com/article/2003/Nov/10/ln/ln01a.html; and "Bethany Hamilton: Persevering after a Shark Attack" by Johanna Skilling, http://www.beliefnet.com/story/137/story_13707.html

3. Carly Boohm as told to Gail Wood, "Don't Let Me Die!" *Campus Life*, Vol. 61, Issue 9 (June/July 2003), 46.

4. Ira Berkow, "It Isn't Whether You Win or Lose . . .," *The New York Times*, 29 October, 2003.

5. Ron Lantz, "Prayer Convoy on Interstate 70," *Guideposts*, September 2003, 41-45.

6. Grace Fox, "The Silver Saint," *Power for Living*, August 3, 2003, 2-6.

7. Grace Fox, "The Circuit Rider," *Power for Living*, September 14, 2003, 1-6.

8. Carolyn Campbell, "Signs of Love," *Ladies' Home Journal*, August 2003, 58-60.

9. Ginnie Graham, "Learning to Walk with Faith," *Tulsa World*, July 26, 2003. A-1, A-3.

10. Lee Knapp, "An After-Christmas Gift," *Christianity Today*, December 2003, 44-45.

11. Elizabeth Gehrman, "Charity's Children," *Good Housekeeping*, June 2003, 160-63, 238.

12. Ray Giunta, "That Boy Was Me," http://www.beliefnet.com/story/120/story_12038.html; Web site accessed 02/06/2004.

13. Rndy Franz, "The Way Out," *Power for Living*, July 27, 2003, 2-6.

14. John W. Kennedy, "Second Chance," *Power for Living*, July 20, 2003, 2-5.

15. Susan G. Hauser, "Till Death Do Us Part," *Ladies' Home Journal*, February 2004, 130-37

16. Kathe Campbell, "Blessing in Reverse," http://www.beliefnet.com/story/120/story_12039.html; Web site accessed 02/06/2004.

17. *This House Saved My Son's Life* by Anne Cassidy. Copyright © June 2003, Reprinted with the permission of *Ladies Home Journal*, Meredith Corporation.

18. Larry Hicks, "Life and Death on Palos Verdes Lake," *Guideposts*, January 2004, 32-36.

19. Bert Ghezzi, "One Friendship at a Time," *Christianity Today*, August 2003, 46-48.

20. Corrie Cutrer, "Finding Purpose in Pain." This article first appeared in *Today's Christian Woman* magazine (January/February 2004), published by Christianity Today International, Carol Stream, Illinois.

21. Mary Ann O'Roark, "Class Act," *Guideposts*, March 2004, 34-35.

22. Joe Portale, "Attacked by Killer Bees," http://www.gp4teens.com/Stories/Article.asp?ID=221&Type=25; Web site accessed 01/29/2004.

23. Ronnie Polaneczky, "Alexandra Scott: She Has Big Dreams for Sick Kids" from an article titled "The 2003 Heroes for Health Awards," *Good Housekeeping*, December 2003, 68, 72.

24. Lisa Collier Cool, "Our Christmas Miracles," *Woman's Day*, 16 December 2003, 62-72.

25. Camilla Bekius, "Is My Sister Going to Die?" *Campus Life*, Vol. 62, No. 5 (November/December 2003), 50.

26. Dr. M.L. Rosvally, "The Dying Drummer Boy," *Power for Living*, June 29, 2003, 2-6.

27. Christin Ditchfield, "Esther Ahn Kim," *Power for Living*, June 27, 2004, 2-6, Based largely on

information from the book titled *If I Perish* (Moody Press, 1977).

28. Elizabeth Gehrman, "The Tender Mercy of Cheryl Kane," *Good Housekeeping*, January 2004, 79-83.

29. James R. Adair, "The Path to Peace," *Power for Living*, August 22, 2004, 2-7.

30. Grace Fox, "Finding Freedom," *Power for Living*, March 7, 2004, 1-6.

31. "Faith on the Frontier," *Power for Living*, December 7, 2003, 2-5.

32. Martha Van Cise, "Widler's World," *Power for Living*, February 27, 2005, 2-7.

33. Eileen Connelly, "I Never Did Forget You," *Good Housekeeping*, October 2003, 66-72.

34. Peter K. Johnson, "Faith Amid the Flames." Reprinted with permission from *Charisma* and *Christian Life*, September 2003. Copyright © Strang Communications Co., USA. All rights reserved. www.charismamag.com.

35. "Kristen Stryker: Planting for Others," http://nationalgardenmonth.org/community/partners/kristen.php; Web site accessed 03/30/2004. Used by permission of the National Gardening Association. www.garden.org.

36. Vicki Huffman, "Once I was Blind," *Power for Living*, November 9, 2003, 2-6.

37. Grace Fox, "Open Door, Open Arms," *Power for Living*, November 30, 2003, 2-5.

38. "Christmas Love," *Power for Living*, December 22, 2002, 2-4.

39. Bradley Winterton, "Chang and Tennis, a Match Made in Heaven," *Teipei Times*, July 27, 2003, 18.

40. "The Moral of the Story" selections were excerpted from *God's Little Devotional Book for Graduates*.

41. Portions of "The End of the Story, Sort of . . ." excerpted from *Be Patient, God Isn't Finished with Me, Yet!*

Additional copies of this title are available
from your local bookstore.

If you have enjoyed this book,
or if it has impacted your life,
we would like to hear from you.

Please contact us at:

Honor Books,
An Imprint of Cook Communications Ministries
4050 Lee Vance View
Colorado Springs, CO 80918
www.cookministries.com

If you come across any great stories that inspire you, we invite you
to share them with us for possible use in future volumes of this
series. You can send them to us at the address below, or e-mail
them to us at
bestinspiration@bordonbooks.com.

Best Inspirational Stories of the Year
c/o Bordon Books
6532 E. 71st Street, Suite 105
Tulsa, OK 74133